...er dreamed of eating your way through New York City? In this tempting recipe-slash-travel journal and guide, Yasmin Newman takes you on a journey to the bright lights of NYC as she tracks down some of the world's most sought-after desserts – and savours them all.

Follow Yasmin's food adventure as she explores NYC's vibrant neighbourhoods, where a plethora of colourful characters and quintessential New York moments add flavour to her experience. She jots down notes, steals photographs and creates a hit list of the best addresses – then dreams up recipes inspired by her favourite New York sweets (and even brings you recipes from iconic New York dessert venues).

The Desserts of New York is *Eat Pray Love* meets NYC, and it's one delicious, cool ride.

The Desserts of New York

To Steve, Inés & Alejo,
who make life even sweeter

The Desserts of New York

AND HOW TO EAT THEM ALL

YASMIN NEWMAN

hardie grant books

Contents

« Hi. I'm Yasmin Newman. And I love desserts. Like, I eat at least one every day, and bake them throughout the week. I love them to the point that I packed up my husband, two-year-old daughter and pregnant self, and relocated from Australia to New York for three months with the sole purpose of eating my way through the city's sweets. It was my 'eat' in an Eat Pray Love dream. Come share the ride. »

Introduction

I once read a book called *The New York Nobody Knows* by a local sociologist who took it upon himself to walk every street of NYC's five boroughs. That's over 10,000 kilometres (6000 miles). He interviewed scores of people during the three-year undertaking and, incidentally, also wore out nine pairs of shoes.

My mission was less vast, but a feat in its own right: in three months, I would eat all of NYC's desserts.** Ninety-one days, 169 venues and 373 desserts to be exact. Or, 4.1 desserts per day. As for the calories, you don't want to know! These stats don't even touch the desserts I created back in my East Village apartment each night, moved by the new tastes and textures still swirling in my mind, so I could relive them with family and friends back home.

According to our sociologist, you have to immerse yourself in the day-to-day to really know a city, and I subscribe to this view. It's out there on the streets, on public transport, in grocery stores and cafes where local life takes place – sometimes, far from tourist attractions – and if you want a city's true flavour, that's where you'll find it.

Food has always been my gateway to somewhere new. True, I'll take any opportunity to eat, particularly dessert, but I appreciate the unsung neighbourhoods, nondescript streets and random alleys a food tip has led me to with equal measure. It's what inspired this trip: chocolate chip cookies, sticky buns and soft serve as my New York passport. Okay, I also really wanted to try *every single one*.

Which brings me to an obvious question: why New York?

Around six years ago, my brother moved from Sydney to the bright lights of Gotham. It's something of a rite of passage for Aussies to live and work abroad and, for many years, London was the go-to. In 2005, the introduction of a new work visa shifted our focus to New York. We've been pouring in ever since, lured by the promise of opportunity and progress, like so many expats and migrants before us.

About the same time, give or take a few years, New York desserts were starting to attract serious global attention. The city, home to top chefs, food magazines

and culinary schools, had long been at the vanguard of culinary innovation. In the dessert department, early foundations were forged with local inventions such as New York cheesecake, Brooklyn blackout cake and black and white cookies. From the 1960s, three million migrants added everything from Jewish bakeries loaded with rugelach and babka to Chinese bun shops peddling custard tarts and Mexican panaderias offering tres leches. By the early 1990s, the first artisan revival was making waves, with new-age bakeries including The City Bakery, Sullivan Street Bakery and Amy's Bread paving the way with organic flours, seasonal market produce and traditional techniques.

> « *I'll take any opportunity to eat, particularly dessert, but I appreciate the unsung neighbourhoods, nondescript streets and random alleys a food tip has led me to with equal measure.* »

But now a fresh crop of pastry chefs imagining desserts in radical forms – from Christina Tosi's infamous compost cookie to Dominique Ansel's game-changing cronut – were adding to the city's solid contingent of sweets, including Magnolia Bakery's cupcakes, whose cameo on *Sex and The City* could be pinpointed as ground zero for the current phenomenon of 'will fly for' sweets. The arrival of social media only fuelled the fanfare for destination desserts, particularly New York's, and copycat renditions were cropping up in cafes and food blogs on the other side of the world. Throw in the next artisan wave stirring in Brooklyn, with venues such as Dough doughnuts, Mast chocolate, Van Leeuwen ice cream and Four & Twenty Blackbirds pies, and NYC was in the ring with Paris for the title of worldwide sweet heavyweight. And, like any self-respecting food lover, I wanted a front row seat.

I also longed to see my brother. Couldn't we hang the expense, stop work and just do it? Live in New York, that is, and eat dessert to our heart's content? It wouldn't be my first food sabbatical (see my book *7000 Islands: A Food Portrait of the Philippines*), but now it wasn't just me – there was my husband Steve, daughter Inés and a baby on the way. We worked out that we could, so we really should, shouldn't we? And so we did.

==

Like all great food, the desserts of New York are a reflection of the city. More than eight million people, well over 100 ethnic groups and around 250 neighbourhoods make up the pulsating metropolis, and every penchant and persuasion can be found in between. From melting pot to avant-garde, old world to cutting edge, global leader to community minded, it's a city of character and contrasts, which is why it appeals to, dare I say, everyone. Just follow one Manhattan thoroughfare through its course – and you should, in the spirit of all great walking cities – to see countless versions of The Big Apple and at least one that speaks to you. Then, sit back and people-watch, in a park or on the subway, and you'll see other traits written in everything from their clothes to their confidence – the quiet disregard for rules, an equal respect for tradition and the freedom to experiment. I came to taste all these qualities in their desserts, and it's a downright delicious mix.

Right now, you could describe NYC as flirting with the past. Molecular is gone, locavore is a given and nostalgia reigns, with layered cakes, rustic pies and soda fountain sundaes found in dedicated purveyors as well as temples of haute cuisine, blurring the line between pop and high culture. The rise of niche producers – not just skilled patissiers and bakers, but specialist doughnut makers,

cupcake purveyors, pie divas, croissant kings and ice-cream cognoscenti – has likewise widened the playing field from the pure restaurant dessert dominion of the past. (As one pastry chef put it: 'New York's finally a bakery town.')

So too have the epic seasonal food markets, including Smorgasburg and Madison Square Eats, and hip food halls, such as Chelsea Market and Union Fare, which have given start-up players, often from outer boroughs, a second outpost and access to Manhattan crowds. The city's greenmarkets (farmers' markets), home to New York State's impeccable produce, have long shaped their sweets and I love how the year can be traced by the calendar of fruits and herbs that fill them.

« *The quiet disregard for rules, an equal respect for tradition and the freedom to experiment. I tasted all these qualities in New York's desserts, and it's a downright delicious mix.* »

You can also see the impact of social media's 'bigger, bolder, better' and lightning speed (Black Tap's wild shakes and the viral rise of rainbow doughnuts are just two examples), and a handful of hybrid or 'frankenfood' creations were

born here (think cronuts and Brooksters). Smash-ups (one classic layered with another, like crème brûlée croissants, or carrot cake doughnuts) is another trend, but New York – the cooler, smarter, most self-assured of the American cities – subdues these OTT tendencies just enough, producing desserts that are playful, technique-driven and crafted from quality ingredients.

Along my way, I chatted with pastry chefs and dessert lovers for their take on the city's sweet beat. Overwhelmingly, it was one of constant inspiration and evolution. And world's best. After all, if you can make it here, you can make it anywhere.

So, if you love sugar, flour, butter, cream and eggs in all their glory, you'll find yourself surrounded by kindred spirits in The Big Apple, a city of serious food lovers who savour doughnuts on their way to work and ice cream on their way home. You'll find fantastic gluten-free and vegan options, but indulgence isn't sacrilege here, at least not where I was. What I witnessed was sweet fervour and dessert joie de vivre: lines pouring out of shops, down sidewalks and around corners; hired clowns entertaining waiting guests; phones snapping sweet scores; and the widest smiles plastered all over faces. If this sounds like you, you'll find yourself right at home in this notebook of mine.

** So, when I say I ate *all* the desserts of New York, I am exaggerating. There are over 50,000 food venues in New York (insane, I know), and you could safely say each has at least one sweet number. But *How to Eat All of the Best Ones* isn't such a catchy book title. And Steve, Inés, my brother Terry, his girlfriend Krista, my best friend Mel and my mum Ruby, plus babe-to-be, all shared the sweet load (tough gig).

So together we ate all the best ones. Well, we did our utmost. In the lead-up to my mission, I prepped like any good operative, scouring every magazine and website for recommendations, and tapping friends and their friends and theirs for the inside word. I prepared a hit list, plotted a map and planned every moment. When we arrived, we threw ourselves in, enjoying dessert for breakfast, lunch and dinner – and in between (my husband excelled in ice-cream eating; my daughter couldn't believe her luck). The thing is, every time we scratched off a venue, we'd catch wind of another. Or a favourite bakery would release a new flavour that we just *had* to try. I returned to New York after I had my baby boy Alejo for one last round, and in the intervening four months, inevitably, a swathe of new places had already cropped up.

So, while this book will take you on a journey from street carts, food trucks, ma and pa joints, hole-in-the-walls and old-school bakeries to hipster joints, cool cafes, chic bars and fine diners, and will feed almost any craving, from classic dishes to wild new inventions, any time day or night (you can have cookies delivered to your apartment at 2.30 am for goodness sake!), it is not exhaustive. I have also kept it to Manhattan and Brooklyn, where most dessert places are found, and I stick mainly to Western sweets. This book was never meant to be hard and fast, rather a starting point for your own sweet food adventure.

For us, it was a once-in-a-lifetime experience – desserts, family and New York City.

How to eat them all

1. **BE DEDICATED.** Divide your time in New York by the number of desserts you want to try. This is your daily goal.

2. **CREATE A GOOGLE MAP.** Plot your hit list of venues, then access it via your phone. It's directions, notebook and nearby dessert locator in one, and will become your most valued tool.

3. **WORK SMART.** Choose a neighbourhood, block out the afternoon and check out all the sweet spots in one hit. Repeat.

4. **SEIZE SPARE MOMENTS.** Watching the Nicks at Madison Square Garden? Detour past Shake Shack. Walking home? Hey, there's dessert down the road. Your venue map becomes particularly handy here (see page 20).

5. **CHECK HOURS OF OPERATION AND MENUS FIRST.** Most restaurants have a different lunch and dinner line up, with the signature typically on at night only. Dessert disappointment is the pits.

6. **GO OFF PEAK.** Arriving before the shop opens, or making a restaurant reservation for late lunch, early dinner or late at night minimises wait time and greatly increases your chance of getting a seat. Also consider deep winter and high summer when queues actually cease to exist.

7. **DINE SOLO.** You can often get a single spot at the counter/bar, and without a reservation. Dessert is the only friend you need.

8. **OR BRING SOMEONE.** You can cover more sweet ground between two (or more) and the memories are really neat.

9. **DRESS WISELY.** Baggy clothes are your allies. And avoiding scales helps. Also, don't think about the calories. You can diet when you're dead.

10. **BE CONSUMED.** Devour *Eater, Time Out, Serious Eats, Grub Street, New York Magazine, The New York Times* and more, and get recommendations from local dessert lovers. In the ever-evolving sweet landscape that is New York, this is just the beginning.

no smoking

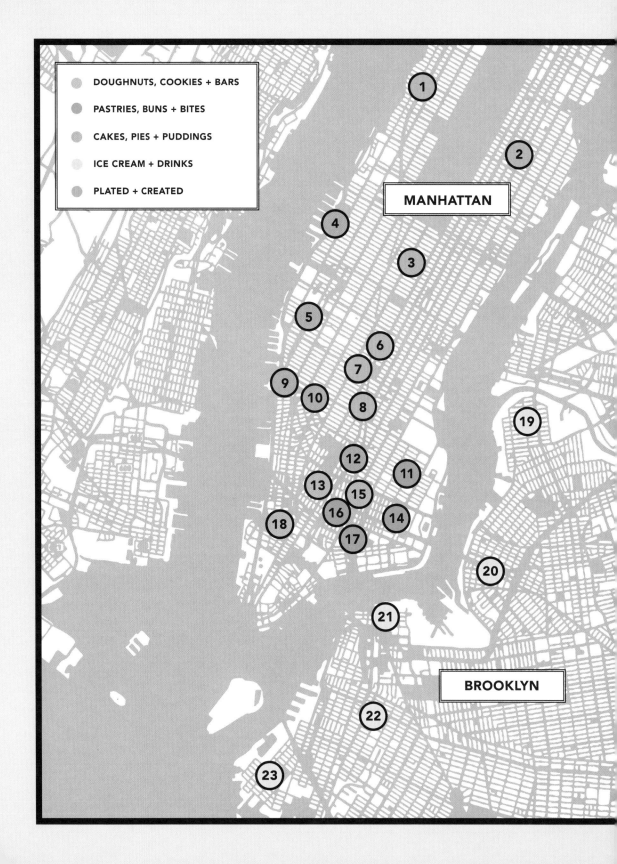

DOUGHNUTS, COOKIES + BARS

PASTRIES, BUNS + BITES

CAKES, PIES + PUDDINGS

ICE CREAM + DRINKS

PLATED + CREATED

MANHATTAN

BROOKLYN

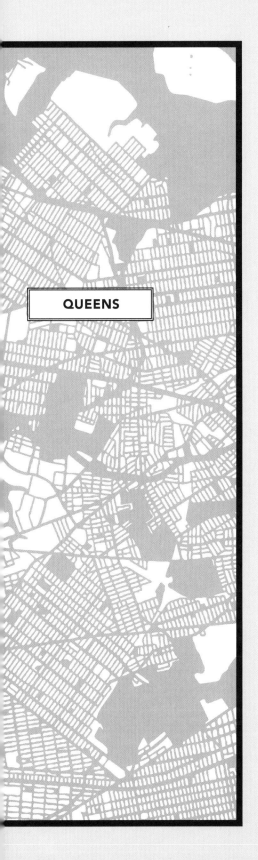

QUEENS

New York neighbourhoods for dessert lovers

1. UPPER WEST SIDE (UWS)
2. UPPER EAST SIDE (UES)
3. MIDTOWN
4. HELL'S KITCHEN
5. CHELSEA/MEATPACKING
6. NOMAD
7. FLATIRON
8. UNION SQUARE
9. WEST VILLAGE
10. GREENWICH VILLAGE
11. EAST VILLAGE
12. NOHO
13. SOHO
14. LOWER EAST SIDE
15. NOLITA
16. LITTLE ITALY
17. CHINATOWN
18. TRIBECA
19. GREENPOINT
20. WILLIAMSBURG
21. DUMBO
22. BOCOCA
23. RED HOOK

«New York changes from block to block, sometimes wildly, and each neighbourhood has its own identity. It's a beautiful kaleidoscope. Desserts often take on the characteristics of their neighbourhood, which is pretty cool, too.»

How to bake like a New Yorker (and use this book)

1. **IT GOES LIKE THIS.** Bake from the recipes, or flip to the end of each chapter for a guide on where to find the best in class. You can also access my interactive map for all the venues listed in these hit lists, plus the extras that didn't fit: www.yasminnewman.com/books/thedessertsofnewyork.

2. **QUALITY IS KING.** Always use the best-quality ingredients you can afford, and local and sustainable where possible. New Yorkers are committed to these ideals, which sets their sweets apart. In general, this means European-style (high-fat – 82%) butter, organic or free-range eggs, unbleached flour, local, organic (not ultra-pasteurised) milk and cream, premium chocolate, seasonal fruit and fresh herbs.

3. **COOKING NOTES.** Unless otherwise stated:

   - Eggs are large (59 g/2 oz).
   - Milk is full-cream (whole).
   - Fine salt is an encompassing term for fine-grain salts such as fine sea salt or kosher salt.
   - Dark chocolate is 55% or 70% cocoa solids as indicated.
   - Vanilla extract is pure.
   - Fruit and vegetables are medium-sized.
   - Light brown sugar is soft brown sugar.
   - Electric mixer is an encompassing term for stand mixers and hand-held electric beaters, used with a whisk, beaters/paddle or dough hook, as indicated. Unless otherwise stated, the mixer is on medium speed.
   - Australian 20 ml (¾ fl oz) tablespoon measures are used in the recipes, so cooks with 15ml (½ fl oz) tablespoons should be generous with their tablespoon measurements.

   - Metric cup measurements are used, i.e. 250 ml (8 ½ fl oz) for 1 cup; in the US a cup is 237 ml (8 fl oz), so American cooks should be generous with their cup measurements; in the UK, a cup is 284 ml (9 ½ fl oz), so British cooks should be scant with their cup measurements.

4. **A SPECIAL NOTE ON CREAM.** It's not always easy to find equivalent creams in different countries, and local labelling can confuse matters further. Here's a rough guide to Australian creams and UK and US substitutions, which are given in the recipes in brackets respectively (when in doubt, look at the fat content listed):

   - *Pouring cream:* a pourable cream with 35% fat. In the UK, substitute whipping cream (35% fat); in the US, heavy cream (38% fat).
   - *Thickened cream:* a thick cream with 35% fat plus stabiliser/gelatine, commonly used to make whipped cream. In the UK and US, substitute whipping cream (35% fat).
   - *Double cream:* a very thick, scoopable cream with 48% fat, typically used for serving. In the UK, substitute extra-thick double cream (48% fat); in the US, clotted cream (55% fat) if available or whipped cream.

5. **SOURCING.** Most ingredients are widely available (there's a recipe note where they're not) and most components are made from scratch. At a pinch, you can substitute store-bought when indicated, and in some recipes the ready-made stuff just works better than homemade (don't get too idealistic).

6. **VARIABLES.** Preparation and bake times vary with local ingredients, humidity, altitude and ovens, so take note of the desired result as much as the indicated times.

7. **FOLLOW SERVING SUGGESTIONS TO A TEE.** In New York, cookies, doughnuts and pastries are baked throughout the day because even a few minutes out of the oven or overnight in the fridge affects the flavour and finish.

8. **WASTE NOT, WANT NOT.** If there's sauce, cream or cake scraps left over, repurpose them in another dish – Christina Tosi's cake truffles came to life this way – or embrace it as an opportunity to lick the bowl.

9. **IF YOU'RE WONDERING,** New York's commercial kitchens often use special equipment and complicated techniques to make desserts just so. These recipes are designed with domestic equipment and the home cook in mind, so they're simpler but retain most of the finesse.

10. **FINALLY.** If there was one tip all of Gotham's sweet artisans would give, it's to read the recipe from top to tail and prep all your ingredients (mise en place) before beginning. Oh, and bake with love.

Doughnuts, cookies & bars

The arrival

DAY 1, DESSERT 1: CAFE AU LAIT DOUGHNUT,
DOUGH, UNION SQUARE

After months of planning, we finally arrived. Hello, New York City! First stop: dessert. It was 9 am, which could only mean doughnuts, 'cause that's what New Yorkers chow on for breakfast. We made a beeline for Dough, nabbed a seat at the counter and ate our giant doughnuts with, wait for it, *plastic cutlery*, just like in an episode of *Seinfeld*. This trip was going to be *so* good.

Classic New York, the one you've grown up with in TV shows and movies, plays out time and again, and it's both thrilling and familiar, from old-school diners and faded bakeshops to stand-up counters and bottomless cups of black coffee. And, just as you'd imagine, doughnuts, cookies and bars are standard and adored.

As we savoured these NYC essentials, one thing became very clear: New Yorkers like their sweets old-school and updated in equal measure. We met cake doughnuts, yeasted doughnuts and doughnut holes ranging from old-fashioned, jelly-filled and crumb-topped to square-shaped, fashioned after layered cakes, glazed with exotica and dyed all the colours of the rainbow. Even Korean doughnuts, hodduk, spilling over with molten brown sugar. Cookies also scaled the spectrum: the circumference of hands, the diameter of tennis balls, loaded with maple bacon, modeled on Oreos or just simple done well: oatmeal raisin, peanut butter, and chocolate chip. Scones championed seasonal fruit and herbs, chunky muffins were topped with cornflake crumbs, and bars explored the holy union of sweet and salty.

New Yorkers also cherish technique. Behind every plain glazed doughnut or kitchen sink cookie, there's obvious know-how with ingredients and the rules they often break.

This was just the first few weeks. It was the most delicious mess I'd ever got myself into.

«We met cake doughnuts, yeasted doughnuts and doughnut holes ranging from old-fashioned, jelly-filled and crumb-topped to square-shaped, fashioned after layered cakes, glazed with exotica and dyed all the colours of the rainbow.»

The glazed doughnuts of your dreams

Years ago, a foodie friend who'd lived in New York raved about the doughnuts, so when I visited not long after, I vowed to eat them all. I hit up LES for Doughnut Plant's epic blackout, tres leches and carrot cake doughnuts, and trekked to Bed-Stuy, when Dough was still just there, for its soft, giant yeasted varieties in hibiscus, lemon meringue and more.

I'd only scratched the surface before I had to leave, and so began the plans, the doughnut seed if you will, for this adventure. Since then, doughnuts have risen to global stardom, but the fried rings of my dreams are still New York's, be they old-fashioned at Peter Pan, new-wave at The Doughnut Project or Korean at Grace Street. You can fill weeks just sampling the selection.

Yeasted doughnuts are the best variety to make at home and these guys are just as you'd find in Gotham: big, billowy and best eaten within a few hours. They're also glazed in tempting flavours, like the three I've included: vanilla bean and halva, dulce de leche and almonds, and fresh cherry. Each makes enough to glaze a dozen doughnuts but if you want to enjoy all three, reduce the quantities accordingly.

Combine the milk and yeast in a bowl and set aside for 5 minutes or until frothy, then whisk in the eggs. Using an electric mixer fitted with the dough hook, knead the flour, sugar, salt, yeast mixture and nutmeg, if using, until combined, then knead for a further 3 minutes. Add the butter, one piece at a time, kneading until incorporated before adding the next, then knead for a further 8–10 minutes or until smooth and elastic (the dough will be quite sticky). Transfer to a large oiled bowl, cover loosely with plastic wrap and set aside in a warm, draught-free place for 2 hours or until doubled in size.

Knock back the dough, then roll it out on a lightly floured work surface until 1.5 cm (½ in) thick. Using a 9 cm (3½ in) concentric doughnut cutter, or 9 cm (3½ in) and 3 cm (1¼ in) round pastry cutters, cut out doughnuts and holes, rerolling the trimmings (you can add the holes to the trimmings or reserve them to cook – my pick). Transfer the doughnuts to two baking trays lined with baking paper, cover loosely with plastic wrap and set aside for 45 minutes or until risen and puffy.

Fill a deep-fryer or large saucepan one-third full of canola oil and heat over medium heat until the temperature reaches 180°C (350°F). Using a flat slotted spoon, gently lower two or three doughnuts into the oil and cook for 45 seconds or until golden underneath. Turn over and cook for a further 45 seconds or until golden and puffed all over. Remove from the oil and drain on paper towel set over a wire rack. Repeat with the remaining doughnuts, returning the oil to 180°C (350°F) between batches.

recipe continued »

MAKES 10–12

200 ml (7 fl oz) lukewarm milk

2 teaspoons dried yeast

2 eggs

500 g (1 lb 2 oz/3⅓ cups) plain (all-purpose) flour

75 g (2¾ oz/⅓ cup) caster (superfine) sugar

1 teaspoon fine salt

pinch of freshly grated nutmeg (optional)

100 g (3½ oz) unsalted butter, chopped, softened

canola oil, to deep-fry

Allow the doughnuts to cool to room temperature then, just before glazing, prepare your choice of glaze. (If you want to try all three, make each one just before glazing.) It should be the consistency of thick, wet sand. If it's too runny, add a little more icing sugar. If it's too thick, warm it a little or add a touch more liquid. Place a wire rack over a tray to catch the drippings.

To make the vanilla halva glaze, whisk the icing sugar, milk and vanilla in a bowl. Add the doughnuts, in batches, and coat generously all over in the glaze, then transfer to the prepared rack. Scatter over the halva and allow to set.

For the dulce de leche and almond glaze, whisk the dulce de leche and boiling water in a bowl until smooth. Add the doughnuts, in batches, and coat generously all over in the glaze, then transfer to the rack. Scatter over the almonds and allow to set.

For the cherry glaze, whisk the icing sugar, smashed cherries and juice in a bowl to combine, pressing the cherry skins to extract as much juice as possible. Add the doughnuts, in batches, and coat generously all over in the glaze, including the cherry skins, then transfer to the rack and allow to set.

TIPS *You can do the legwork on these doughnuts the day before, then finish off the next day by proving the dough in the fridge – overnight for the first rise, and for 2½ hours for the second. For doughnut holes, reduce the cooking time to 30 seconds per side. Cool slightly, then coat generously in caster (superfine) or icing (confectioners') sugar, or in your choice of glaze if you have any left over.*

VANILLA BEAN + HALVA GLAZE
300 g (10½ oz/2 cups) pure icing (confectioners') sugar, sifted

1½ tablespoons warm milk

1 teaspoon vanilla bean paste

crumbled halva, to scatter

DULCE DE LECHE + TOASTED ALMOND GLAZE
395 g (14 oz) dulce de leche (see tip, page 174)

2 tablespoons boiling water

toasted flaked almonds, to scatter

FRESH CHERRY GLAZE
300 g (10½ oz/2 cups) pure icing (confectioners') sugar

90 g (3 oz) pitted fresh cherries, smashed, juices reserved

Peter Pan Donut & Pastry Shop

*Peter Pan Donut & Pastry Shop is consistently full. Greenpoint used to be a
Polish neighbourhood and although it's gentrified, you'll still see old-timers in the shop.
People sit down for coffee, or buy up boxes of old-fashioned and glazed, which are
tied up with retro red and white string that hangs from the ceiling. It's been the same
recipe for over sixty years, and doughnuts are only $1.10 a pop.*

Soho

Short for South of Houston Street – and synonymous with shopping. Broadway is madness, but the side-street boutiques make you wish you could afford something.

I've scored Dominique Ansel's cronuts on two occasions, something a New York friend has never managed. The trick is to arrive before the bakery opens. I guess I'm just more dedicated.

The buildings on Greene and Mercer have the most incredible cast-iron facades, vast windows and soaring ceilings. They were built for manufacturing before the artists, then retailers moved in.

Black & white cookie, as explained by Seinfeld

'The key to eating a black and white cookie, Elaine, is you want to get some black and some white in each bite,' says Seinfeld. 'Nothing mixes better than vanilla and chocolate. And yet, still, somehow racial harmony still eludes us. If people would only look to the cookie. All our problems would be solved.'

('THE DINNER PARTY.' *SEINFELD*. NBC.)

Giant snickerdoodles

Late one Tuesday night, around 2.30 am, the apartment buzzer beeped and my brother's girlfriend, Krista, popped out of their room to open the door. 'I ordered cookies,' she said, equally sheepish and excited. A few minutes later, there was a box filled with warm, just-baked cookies sitting on our table, brimming with choc chips, oatmeal and raisins, and something I'd never heard of before: snickerdoodles. I *love* American dessert names.

The snickerdoodle (a classic, I've since learned) and I have been best buds ever since. Its soft, chewy texture, intense buttery flavour and crackly cinnamon-sugar crust is perfect for midnight cookie cravings, or whenever you want something moreish but not too rich. So any time, really.

It's one of those sweets that tastes so good you think there must be more to it, but it's easy as. These are inspired by the oversized cookies you find all over New York and, in the city that never sleeps, can even have delivered to your door.

Sift the flour, cream of tartar, bicarbonate of soda and salt into a bowl. Mix the cinnamon and 55 g (2 oz/¼ cup) of the sugar in a separate bowl, then set both bowls aside.

Using an electric mixer, beat the butter and remaining 220 g (8 oz/1 cup) sugar for 3 minutes or until light and creamy. Add the egg and beat until well combined, then beat in the vanilla. Add the flour mixture and beat on low speed until just combined. Scatter over half the cinnamon sugar, then beat once to just swirl through. Shape into eight balls then, working with one ball at a time, coat well in the remaining cinnamon sugar. Refrigerate for 20 minutes to firm slightly.

Preheat the oven to 180°C (350°F) and line two baking trays with baking paper.

Place the cookie balls, 8 cm (3¼ in) apart, on the prepared baking trays. Bake the cookies, one tray at a time, for 10–12 minutes or until just golden around the edges (they will be slightly undercooked in the centre). Remove from the oven and cool slightly on the trays, then transfer to a wire rack to cool completely.

TIP *Bake 12 smaller cookies and sandwich them together with vanilla ice cream. Mmm …*

MAKES 8

225 g (8 oz/1½ cups) plain (all-purpose) flour

1 teaspoon cream of tartar

½ teaspoon bicarbonate of soda (baking soda)

⅛ teaspoon fine salt

1½ teaspoons ground cinnamon

275 g (9½ oz/1¼ cups) caster (superfine) sugar

150 g (5½ oz) unsalted butter, chopped, softened

1 egg

1 teaspoon natural vanilla extract

Burnt butter chocolate chip cookies

If there's one cookie that gets New York's heart racing, it's the chocolate chip. You could say that about a lot of places, but the sheer number of iterations here, the cult followings they attract, and the outrageous quantities sold daily, well, it takes the cookie.

There's also the taste – Gotham's are the best (and I consider myself an authority on this as I've consumed a fair few in my lifetime). Highlights include Maman's, loaded with three nuts, Almondine Bakery's discs with milk and dark chocolate, and Levain Bakery's – perhaps the city's most loved version – in all its insane tennis-ball-size, gooey-interior glory.

I don't want to call favourites, and I'm not, but this recipe takes inspiration from Levain's unique approach to *size*, weighing in at over 120 g (4½ oz), making it a meal-slash-cookie. Instead of creaming, I've browned the butter, giving a wonderfully nutty edge. Make sure you eat them 10–15 minutes after they come out of the oven, when they're just set and perfect.

Place the butter in a saucepan over low–medium heat until melted and starting to foam. Cook, stirring occasionally, for a further 12–15 minutes or until the butter is browned and has a nutty aroma. Remove from the heat and leave to cool.

Sift the flour, bicarbonate of soda and salt into a bowl and set aside. Using an electric mixer, beat the burnt butter and sugars in a large bowl for 1 minute or until well combined (it will look like wet sand). Add the eggs and vanilla and beat until well combined. Add the flour mixture and beat on low speed until just combined, then stir in the chocolate and walnuts.

Line two baking trays with baking paper. Divide the dough into ten even portions and shape into balls, then place, 5 cm (2 in) apart, on the prepared trays and refrigerate for 2 hours or until very firm.

Preheat the oven to 180°C (350°F).

Bake the cookies, one tray at a time, for 18 minutes or until just golden around the edges (the dough will be slightly gooey on the inside). Remove from the oven and cool slightly on the trays, then transfer to a wire rack to cool for a further 10 minutes. Serve immediately.

MAKES 10

125 g (4½ oz) unsalted butter, chopped

375 g (13 oz/2½ cups) plain (all-purpose) flour

½ teaspoon bicarbonate of soda (baking soda)

1 teaspoon fine salt

165 g (6 oz/¾ cup) caster (superfine) sugar

165 g (6 oz/¾ cup firmly packed) light brown sugar

2 eggs

1 teaspoon natural vanilla extract

200 g (7 oz) dark chocolate (55% cocoa solids), cut into 1 cm (½ in) pieces

100 g (3½ oz/1 cup) walnuts, toasted, halved

TIPS *If the cookies cool and harden, warm them slightly in a low oven or in the microwave and they'll spring back to life (it's all about the melted chocolate and cookie goo). You can also freeze the dough balls and bake them when you're ready.*

Luxe Oreos

In 1912, the National Biscuit Company in New York released the Oreo, aka everyone's secret pleasure and the best-selling packaged cookie of all time. Production no longer takes place at the original facility (the building is now Chelsea Market, one of New York's best food halls), but the Oreo's connection to the city lives on in the many sweet odes found across town.

At Bouchon Bakery, Thomas Keller's TKO (with its cheeky double entendre) is probably the most famous, although Maman offers a new frontrunner. Then there's the scores of inspired desserts, including NoMad's much-loved cookies and cream balls.

These cookies combine deep, dark chocolate shortbread with a decadent vanilla-flecked mascarpone cream centre, and are larger and prettier than the original – so everything you love about Oreos, just luxe.

Preheat the oven to 160°C (320°F) and line two baking trays with baking paper.

Sift the flour, cocoa powder, bicarbonate of soda and salt into a bowl and set aside. Using an electric mixer, beat the butter and sugar in a large bowl for 3 minutes or until light and creamy. Add the flour mixture and beat on low speed until the dough just comes together. Shape into two discs, then wrap one in plastic wrap and refrigerate until needed.

Roll out the remaining dough between two sheets of baking paper until 3 mm (⅛ in) thick. Using a 7 cm (2¾ in) round cookie cutter, cut out rounds, rerolling the trimmings, and place on the prepared trays, 3 cm (1¼ in) apart. Using a 6 cm (2½ in) fluted cookie cutter, make an indent in the centre of the cookies to decorate, if desired.

Bake, swapping the trays halfway through, for 15 minutes or until the cookies are just cooked (it's difficult to tell from the dark colour, but there may be small cracks on top). Remove from the oven and cool completely on the trays. Repeat with the remaining dough to make 40 cookies all up.

Meanwhile, to make the mascarpone vanilla cream, place all the ingredients in a bowl and whisk with an electric mixer until stiff peaks form.

Take 20 of the cookies and spread 1½ tablespoons of the mascarpone cream over the flat side of each cookie, then sandwich with the remaining cookies. Cover and refrigerate for 3 hours or until the mascarpone cream is firm. Serve chilled or at room temperature. The cookies will keep in an airtight container in the fridge for up to 3 days.

MAKES 20

- 260 g (9 oz/1¾ cups) plain (all-purpose) flour
- 150 g (5½ oz/1½ cups) unsweetened (Dutch) cocoa powder
- ½ teaspoon bicarbonate of soda (baking soda)
- ½ teaspoon fine salt
- 250 g (9 oz) unsalted butter, chopped, softened
- 220 g (8 oz/1 cup) caster (superfine) sugar

MASCARPONE VANILLA CREAM
- 250 g (9 oz) mascarpone
- 125 ml (4 fl oz/½ cup) thickened (whipping) cream
- 150 g (5½ oz/1 cup) pure icing (confectioners') sugar, sifted
- 1 teaspoon vanilla bean paste

Baked's Brooksters

Let me get this right: it's a brownie *and* a chocolate chip cookie, so basically two of my favourite sweets in one? That was my reaction when I first met the Brookster and, as I later learned from the co-creators, pretty much everyone's 'say what?' response.

Matt Lewis and Renato Poliafito came up with it back in 2008, long before hybrid desserts were in, and the inspired creation has been a fixture at their perennially popular Brooklyn bakery, Baked, ever since. They kindly shared this recipe with me from *Baked Elements: Our 10 Favorite Ingredients* (Stewart, Tabori & Chang), one of their best-selling cookbooks and a personal favourite, plus an extra note for you:

'This recipe is fairly straightforward, but requires time. Don't rush the specified times as it's important for the dough and batter to cool and thicken slightly for a perfect bake.'

I've also tried this warmed slightly in a sundae and it's the best foundation you can imagine.

To make the chocolate chip cookie filling, whisk the flour, bicarbonate of soda and salt in a large bowl and set aside. Using an electric mixer, beat the butter and sugars on medium speed until smooth and creamy. Scrape down the sides and bottom of the bowl. Add the eggs, one at a time, beating well after each addition (the mixture will look light and fluffy). Add the vanilla and beat for 5 seconds. Add half the flour mixture and beat for 15 seconds, then add the remaining flour mixture and beat until just combined. Fold in the chocolate chips until evenly combined. Cover the bowl tightly with plastic wrap and refrigerate for 3 hours.

To make the brownie shells, grease six individual 10 cm (4 in) pie dishes and place on a baking tray. Whisk the flour, cocoa and salt in a bowl and set aside. Place the chocolate and butter in a heatproof bowl set over a saucepan of gently simmering water (don't let the bowl touch the water) and stir occasionally until melted and combined. Remove from the heat, but keep the bowl over the water in the saucepan. Add both sugars and whisk until well combined. Remove the bowl from the water and cool to room temperature.

Add the eggs to the chocolate mixture, one at a time, whisking after each addition until just combined, then stir in the vanilla (do not overbeat the batter at this stage or the brownies will be cakey). Sprinkle the flour mixture over the chocolate mixture, then using a spatula (do not use a whisk), fold in until there is just a trace amount of flour mixture visible. Fill the pie dishes with the brownie batter until just under halfway full. Refrigerate for 3 hours.

MAKES 6

280 g (10 oz) plain (all-purpose) flour

1 teaspoon bicarbonate of soda (baking soda)

1 teaspoon fine salt

225 g (8 oz) unsalted butter, chopped, softened

200 g (7 oz) dark brown sugar

100 g (3½ oz) caster (superfine) sugar

2 eggs

2 teaspoons natural vanilla extract

340 g (12 oz) dark chocolate chips

ice cream, to serve (optional)

BROWNIE SHELLS

95 g (3¼ oz) plain (all-purpose) flour

3 teaspoons unsweetened (Dutch) cocoa powder

½ teaspoon fine salt

140 g (5 oz) dark chocolate (60–72% cocoa solids), roughly chopped

115 g (4 oz) unsalted butter, chopped

150 g (5½ oz) caster (superfine) sugar

50 g (1¾ oz) light brown sugar

3 eggs

1 teaspoon natural vanilla extract

Preheat the oven to 190°C (375°F).

To assemble the Brooksters, using an ice-cream scoop with a release mechanism, scoop cookie dough into ¼ cup-sized balls then, using your hands, shape the dough into perfect balls. Gently flatten each ball into a disc (the discs should be slightly smaller than the tops of the pie dishes). Gently press a cookie dough disc into the brownie batter in each pie dish. (You may have leftover cookie batter, which you can scoop into 1½ tablespoon-sized balls and bake on a separate baking tray.)

Place the baking tray in the oven and bake, rotating the tray halfway through, for 20–25 minutes or until the cookie part is golden brown. Cool to room temperature or serve warm with ice cream, if desired.

BAKED'S TIP *You can also bake smaller Brooksters in a standard 12-cup muffin or cupcake tin with these modifications: use a light-coloured tin as dark-coloured metal will cause the edges to crisp up too early. Decrease the oven temperature to 180°C (350°F). Rotate the tin halfway through and make sure the Brooksters don't overbake; they will probably take slightly longer as they are thicker.*

Nolita

As in North of Little Italy. Or Soho's edgier sibling. It's one of the coolest 'hoods.

My brother works nearby, so we often met here for lunch, then grabbed Rices to Riches for dessert. He's always loved rice pudding.

La Esquina is my favourite Nolita landmark. It's part taqueria, restaurant and speakeasy housed in a rad, old-school-looking deli. Plus, I can't get enough of Mexican.

The mod bakeshop

I'd often pass by Christina Tosi's original Milk Bar in East Village on my way home;
I just can't get enough of her b'day truffles. One time, it was almost midnight. A thick
crowd jostled out the front, and drum and base was pumping. I almost mistook it
for a cool gig, save for everyone eating soft serve, cake and pie.

Katherine, food editor

'In my opinion, one of New York's best bakeries is Bakeri in Brooklyn. I love to sit in the front window of the Williamsburg location and people watch, or in the back garden on a sunny day. My absolute favourite are their salted caramel brownies. They're chewy, moist, decadently chocolatey and delicious. They're served in little squares or as regular brownies, but do yourself a favour and get the full size. They are so good.'

Tribeca

Derived from Triangle Below Canal. A bunch of celebrities live here, which I wouldn't ordinarily care about, but we're talking about Beyonce and Jay-Z.

French street artist JR's mural at Franklin and Church (above) is one of the city's best. It's based on a 1900s archival photo of child immigrants being processed at Ellis Island, and is haunting.

I popped into Baked Tribeca all the time. There's always something new to try and it's always really good. They've really nailed the whole modern American bakeshop thing.

Tres leches cake balls

I have a few New York dessert heroes and Christina Tosi is one of them. Among other things, she champions leftovers, such as cake cuttings, which she turns into cake truffles (delicious balls of moistened cake coated in white chocolate and sweet crumbs). Without fail, I'd grab a pack of b'day truffles every time I walked home past Milk Bar in East Village. They are – and I can't believe I'm making this call – my favourite New York dessert (well, at least in the top five).

These cake balls are inspired by another flavour combination cherished in New York – the Mexican three-milk cake known as tres leches. At Doughnut Plant, the classic is reimagined as epic tres leches cake doughnuts, while Empellón Cocina serves a chocolate tres leches special. Here, they're just spiced, smooth as chocolate ganache and dusted in sweet milk powder.

Preheat the oven to 180°C (350°F). Grease a round 20 cm (8 in) springform tin and line the base with baking paper.

Sift the flour, baking powder and salt into a bowl and set aside. Using an electric mixer, whisk the eggs, sugar and vanilla for 10 minutes or until light and tripled in volume. In two batches, alternately add the flour mixture and milk, whisking on low speed until just combined. Pour the batter into the prepared tin and bake for 30–35 minutes or until the centre of the cake springs back when gently touched. Remove from the oven and let the cake cool completely in the tin.

To make tres leches soak, place all the ingredients in a bowl and whisk to combine. Set aside.

Remove the cooled cake from the tin and, using a large serrated knife, trim the top, bottom and sides so only the white centre remains. Tear the cake centre into pieces, place in a food processor and process to fine crumbs. Pour over the tres leches soak and process until very smooth, adding an extra 1 tablespoon cream if necessary (you want the mixture to be moist but firm enough to roll into a ball). Refrigerate for 1 hour to firm slightly.

Combine the milk powder and icing sugar in one bowl and place the melted white chocolate in a separate bowl. Roll the cake mixture into 3–4 cm (1¼–1½ in) balls. Working with one ball at a time, coat in a thin layer of chocolate, using your fingers to spread it evenly, then coat generously in the milk powder mixture, shaking off the excess. Cover and refrigerate for 3 hours for the chocolate to set and the flavours to infuse. Serve chilled or at room temperature. The balls will keep in an airtight container in the fridge for up to 1 week.

MAKES ABOUT 15

225 g (8 oz/1½ cups) plain (all-purpose) flour

2 teaspoons baking powder

½ teaspoon fine salt

3 eggs

220 g (8 oz/1 cup) caster (superfine) sugar

2 teaspoons natural vanilla extract

125 ml (4 fl oz/½ cup) milk

2 tablespoons milk powder

2 tablespoons pure icing (confectioners') sugar

120 g (4½ oz) white chocolate, melted

TRES LECHES SOAK

80 ml (2½ fl oz/⅓ cup) evaporated milk

80 ml (2½ fl oz/⅓ cup) pouring (whipping/heavy) cream, plus extra if needed

125 ml (4 fl oz/½ cup) sweetened condensed milk

1 tablespoon natural vanilla extract

¼ teaspoon ground cinnamon

pinch of ground cloves

Fig & Marsala glazed scones

I'm a die-hard fan of traditional British scones served with sweet jam and whipped cream, but I've also come to love America's take: generous, wedge-shaped and chunky with mix-ins. They're also typical breakfast fare – not just afternoon tea – which is a *major* plus.

With unique flavour combinations that mirror the seasons, New York scones are particularly captivating. In summer, you'll find blackberry and mint at Ovenly, while in winter Bibble & Sip turns out a mean spiced pear with bergamot glaze. Then there's the constant favourite at Levain studded with oatmeal and raisins.

These scones, made with dried figs plumped up in sweet Marsala, can be enjoyed year round, and the syrup doubles as a glaze, which makes them even more lush.

To make the Marsala figs, place the Marsala, sugar and water in a small saucepan and bring to the boil over medium–high heat, stirring to dissolve the sugar. Add the figs and cook, stirring occasionally, for 8–10 minutes or until syrupy. Remove from the heat and set aside to cool.

Place the flour, sugar, baking powder, salt and lemon zest in a large bowl. Remove the figs from the syrup, reserving the syrup, then add the figs to the flour mixture and toss to combine. Pour in the cream and honey and stir until just combined. Shape into a rustic 20 cm (8 in) round (don't flatten it, it's supposed to have a bit of height), cover with plastic wrap and refrigerate for 30 minutes to firm slightly.

Preheat the oven to 200°C (400°F) and line a baking tray with baking paper.

Cut the dough into eight equal wedges, then place, 5 cm (2 in) apart, on the prepared tray (the dough may be a bit sticky and tricky to move, so don't worry if the wedges become slightly misshapen). Bake for 15 minutes or until golden and risen.

Remove the scones from the oven and, while they are still warm, brush with the reserved glaze (you may have some glaze left over). Cool for 20 minutes, then serve warm (my pick) or at room temperature (just as good!).

MAKES 8

300 g (10½ oz/2 cups) plain (all-purpose) flour

2 tablespoons caster (superfine) sugar

1 tablespoon baking powder

½ teaspoon fine salt

finely grated zest of 1 large lemon

330 ml (11 fl oz/1⅓ cups) thickened (whipping) cream

1 tablespoon honey

MARSALA FIGS

125 ml (4 fl oz/½ cup) Marsala

110 g (4 oz/½ cup) caster (superfine) sugar

125 ml (4 fl oz/½ cup) water

100 g (3½ oz) dried figs, stalks removed, quartered

Key lime bars (kinda)

To me, 'key lime', named for the Florida Keys where the genus of citrus once grew abundantly, has always had an exotic ring to it. So it was with great anticipation that I tried my first key lime pie, in Red Hook, Brooklyn no less, where Steve's Authentic has been turning out the American southern speciality for twenty years. The pie was tangy, silky and crumbly, and I was an instant devotee, joining the bands of New Yorkers who go gaga for the combo. (You can find everything from key lime macarons to doughnuts, too.)

Also known as Mexican limes, key limes differ from regular Persian limes in tartness and flavour. You could loosely describe it as lime with a dash of lemon, which is what you can substitute if you can't get your hands on the real stuff (which can be hard, particularly abroad). It's also what I've used in these key lime-inspired bars with the most delicious lime-lemon curd and a crust so short and buttery it nearly disintegrates on contact.

Grease a 23 cm (9 in) square cake tin and line with baking paper.

To make the shortcrust base, using an electric mixer, beat the butter and icing sugar for 2 minutes or until light and creamy. Add the flour and salt, and beat on low speed until just combined. Transfer to the tin then, using an offset spatula or your hands, press the mixture evenly over the base (I place a piece of baking paper on top to help). Refrigerate for 1 hour to firm.

Preheat the oven to 180°C (350°F).

Bake the base for 18 minutes or until golden, then reduce the oven temperature to 150°C (300°F).

Meanwhile, whisk the eggs, egg yolks, sugar, juices and zest in a saucepan until well combined. Set the pan over medium heat, add the butter and whisk until melted and combined. Cook, whisking constantly, for a further 8 minutes or until thickened and the mixture almost comes to the boil. Remove from the heat and whisk in the cream.

Pour the lemon and lime curd through a sieve over the base and bake the slice for 13–15 minutes or until just cooked around edges (it should still have a slight wobble in the centre).

Remove the slice from the oven and cool for 1 hour, then carefully remove the slice from the tin. Cut it into 20 even rectangles and serve at room temperature (for a melt-in-your mouth crust). Alternatively, cover and refrigerate for 2 hours or until cold, and serve chilled. The bars will keep in an airtight container in the fridge for up to 1 week. (Warm them briefly in the microwave if you want to achieve that super short crust again.)

MAKES 20

2 eggs
4 egg yolks
295 g (10½ oz/1⅓ cups) caster (superfine) sugar
125 ml (4 fl oz/½ cup) lime juice
60 ml (2 fl oz/¼ cup) lemon juice
finely grated zest of 1 lime
finely grated zest of ½ lemon
125 g (4 oz) unsalted butter, chopped, softened
60 ml (2 fl oz/¼ cup) thickened (whipping) cream

SHORTCRUST BASE
200 g (7 oz) unsalted butter, softened, chopped
75 g (2¾ oz/½ cup) icing (confectioners') sugar
200 g (7 oz/1⅓ cups) plain (all-purpose) flour
⅛ teaspoon fine salt

Green tea sablés

I never cared for matcha or green tea desserts until I tried it New York style. The on-trend ingredient just didn't work for me in the cakes, cookies, crêpes etc. I'd previously eaten. Then, a green tea ice cream at Patisserie Tomoko took me by surprise; its dialed-down sweetness allowed the complex matcha to shine. Later, at Burrow, roasted green tea known as hojicha replaced the favoured green tea powder in a crisp, buttery cookie that, too, was just sweet. Magic.

I've championed longjing (dragon well), my go-to morning green, in these beautiful French sablés, but you can use any good-quality green tea leaves (except from tea bags), which you toast, then loosely grind. They're light, exotic and an alluring shade of light green – and perfect for a picnic in Central or Washington Square Park.

Toast the tea leaves in a small frying pan over medium–high heat for 3 minutes or until fragrant. Cool, then grind quite finely in a spice grinder or small food processor (don't take it as far as a powder though – you still want a little texture there).

Grease a 32 cm (12¾ in) × 22 cm (8¾ in) rectangular cake tin and line with baking paper. Using an electric mixer, beat the butter and sugars for 3 minutes or until light and creamy. Add the egg yolks and vanilla and beat until well combined. Add the flour, salt and ground tea, and beat on low speed until just combined. Transfer to the tin and then, using an offset spatula or your hands, press the mixture evenly over the base (I place a piece of baking paper on top to help). Refrigerate for 30 minutes to firm.

Preheat the oven to 180°C (350°F).

Scatter the top generously with the raw sugar. Bake for 18 minutes or until golden. Cool completely, then cut into 24 pieces to serve.

MAKES 24

2½ tablespoons longjing, sencha or other green tea leaves

250 g (9 oz) unsalted butter, chopped, softened

110 g (4 oz/½ cup) caster (superfine) sugar

35 g (1¼ oz/⅓ cup) icing (confectioners') sugar, sifted

2 egg yolks

2 teaspoons natural vanilla extract

300 g (10½ oz/2 cups) plain (all-purpose) flour

¼ teaspoon fine salt

raw (demerara) sugar, for scattering

WASHINGTON
SQUARE PARK
14.38

Doughnuts with Fany Gerson, Dough

LOW + SLOW

Don't be tempted to put dough in a warm place to speed things up. If you retard proving for as long as you can, you'll get the best result.

SECRET TOUCH

Flavour the dough, whether with lemon zest, nutmeg or cinnamon (make sure to use fresh). You won't taste it – it's like seasoning – but it makes all the difference.

WELL OILED

Use a neutral-tasting oil with a high smoke point (such as canola) to prevent burning and imparting flavour. Cool, drain and reuse your oil, too.

EASY DOES IT

People often throw their doughnuts into the oil 'cause they're nervous, but get close and just slide them in.

Rainbow doughnut

When The Bagel Store's rainbow bagels went viral, Moe's Doughs got an idea.

OLD-FASHIONED CAKE DOUGHNUT BASE + BATTERS TINTED WITH FOOD COLOURING,

THEN SWIRLED BEFORE FRYING + VANILLA GLAZE

Hello, rainbow doughnut!

DON'T LITTER

9–10:30AM
TUES
&
FRI

WILLIAMSBURG
12.49

Hit List

Doughnut shops

Dough

448 LAFAYETTE AVE, BROOKLYN (BED-STUY);
14 W 19TH ST, NEW YORK (FLATIRON).

The giant yeasted doughnuts at Fany Gerson's much-loved Dough (she's also behind La Newyorkina; see *Ice Cream*, page 184) come slathered in glistening glaze and crunchy toppings, from cafe au lait (my fave) to blood orange (another one), and are among New York's all-time finest. The filled doughnuts, such as lemon with scorched meringue, are worthy of all the hype, too.

Doughnut Plant

379 GRAND ST, NEW YORK (LES);
PLUS THREE MORE LOCATIONS.

You can thank Mark Israel for crème brûlée doughnuts, square doughnuts and cake doughnuts in tres leches, blackout and carrot cake. Personally, I can't get enough of them. His inventions have garnered a global following (plus plenty of knock offs) but none come close to the originals, and he nails both cake and yeasted varieties, which few competitors can claim.

Doughnuttery

CHELSEA MARKET, 425 W 15TH ST, NEW YORK (CHELSEA);
PLUS TWO MORE LOCATIONS.

If you're into little things, you'll love Doughnuttery, which specialises in doughnuts smaller than your palm. The mini rings are fried in front of you, then doused in creative sugars, from Flower Power (hibiscus, honey and rose petals) to PBCP (peanut butter, cayenne pepper and pretzels), and served with equally outlandish dipping sauces, such as beer caramel.

Dun-Well Doughnuts

222 MONTROSE AVE, BROOKLYN (EAST WILLIAMSBURG);
102 ST MARKS PLACE, NEW YORK (EAST VILLAGE).

Vegans, rejoice, then head to New York's first all-vegan doughnut shop for yeasted, cake and filled rings in flavours from pumpkin spice and Boston cream to biscotti and lavender butter. I'm not vegan, but I hear they rock.

Moe's Doughs Donut Shop

126 NASSAU AVE, BROOKLYN (GREENPOINT).

Following the social media splash of rainbow bagels in early 2016, multicoloured just-about-everything started appearing, including rainbow doughnuts at Moe's Doughs. They don't look like much from the outside, but take a bite and a swirl of colour welcomes you, and the taste, even if it's just a glazed vanilla cake doughnut, is pretty good, too.

Peter Pan Donut & Pastry Shop

727 MANHATTAN AVE, BROOKLYN (GREENPOINT).

Sixty years on, this Greenpoint institution pumps daily, with queues for boxes of takeaway doughnuts, or a seat to eat in. Head here for a bargain (fried treats are only $1.10 each!), classic styles like old-fashioned and jelly, and genuine old-school charm. Go for the red velvet cake and honey dip yeasted doughnuts.

The Doughnut Project

10 MORTON ST, NEW YORK (WEST VILLAGE).

A relative newcomer (and fast local favourite), this West Village purveyor excels in giant yeasted doughnuts in inspired flavours. Think olive oil and black pepper or the beetroot-glazed, ricotta-filled Those Beetz are Dope. While delicious savoury adaptations are a common theme, classic reimaginings are also stellar, including my fave, Peanut Butter Jelly Time.

OTHER NOTABLES: Mike's Donuts, Orwasher's Bakery, The Donut Pub, Underwest Doughnuts.

Bakeries, patisseries & cafes

Almondine Bakery

85 WATER ST, BROOKLYN (DUMBO).

This traditional French patisserie-cafe also makes a chocolate chip cookie à l'Américaine. The colossal round, laden with pieces of smooth European milk chocolate and a smattering of rich dark chocolate on top, is chewy rather than crisp or undercooked. It bucks the usual NYC trend and, as such, is one of my choc chip picks.

Baked

359 VAN BRUNT ST, BROOKLYN (RED HOOK);
279 CHURCH ST, NEW YORK (TRIBECA).

If there's a tout worth mentioning, it's one from Oprah, who praised the new-age American bakeshop's brownies (go the Sweet + Salty). I fell so hard for their Brooksters – half cookie, half brownie – I asked for owners Matt and Renato's recipe (page 40). The lemon-lime bars are all-time, too. (Also, see *Cakes*, page 144.)

Bibble & Sip

253 W 51ST ST, NEW YORK (MIDTOWN).

In the sweet dessert land that is Midtown West is new kid on the block Bibble & Sip. The cafe-cum-patisserie is of French/Asian/American leaning, with delicious mash-ups like matcha panna cotta and PB&J milk buns (see *Buns*, page 102). The seasonal scones, in flavours such as spiced pear with earl grey glaze, are up there with the city's best.

Birdbath Bakery

160 PRINCE ST, NEW YORK (SOHO);
PLUS SIX MORE LOCATIONS.

Chocolate chip cookies – oversized, crunchy and chewy – are the sweet speciality at Birdbath, the small-scale eco offshoot of City Bakery, whose signature pretzel croissants and breakfast muffins are also for sale. Inside tip: the Soho flagship resides in a former Italian bakery with charming original signage, so look for Vesuvio Bakery instead of Birdbath.

Bouchon Bakery

TIME WARNER CENTER, 10 COLUMBUS CIRCLE,
NEW YORK (UWS); ROCKEFELLER CENTRE,
1 ROCKEFELLER PLAZA, NEW YORK (MIDTOWN).

Thomas Keller's bakery began life in Napa Valley, but his two New York locations are local institutions and people come in droves for his luxurious takes on American cookie classics: the TKO (Thomas Keller Oreo), TLC (a pecan twist on oatmeal and raisin) and Better Nutters (upgraded Nutter Butters).

Breads Bakery

18 E 16TH ST, NEW YORK (FLATIRON);
1890 BROADWAY, NEW YORK (UWS).

The chocolate Nutella babka and rugelach (see *Pastries*, page 102) may reign supreme, but this cool bakery-meets-canteen serving up artisan breads and baked goods with Israeli influences also makes a mean brownie and reverse chocolate chip cookies with white, milk and dark choc chunks and a chewy finish.

Burrow

68 JAY ST, BROOKLYN (DUMBO).

In a Brooklyn version of *Alice in Wonderland* comes Burrow, a teeny tiny pastry shop filled with decidedly delicate and pretty little sweets. A French and Japanese persuasion inform the array, from palmier and kouign amann to cotton-soft cheesecake (see *Cakes*, page 145) and the must-try roasted green tea biscuits. It's also hidden in the lobby of an office building.

Glaser's Bake Shop

1670 1ST AVENUE, NEW YORK (UES).

Head here for real-deal black and white cookies and a side of nostalgia, which comes free with each giant (15 cm/6 in!) round slathered with chocolate and vanilla frosting (just $1.60 each!). Glaser's has been in business for 115 years and by the looks of the friendlier-than-ever white-haired staff, you may even be served by the original team.

Grace Street

17 W 32ND ST, NEW YORK (MIDTOWN).

It's not all-American doughnuts winning hearts in NYC. Grace Street, a pumping coffee shop in the heart of Koreatown, serves up hodduk to constant crowds. The warm dough pockets oozing brown sugar and walnuts is a South Korean speciality, served here with an optional scoop of vanilla ice cream (do it). Black sesame shaved snow is another winner.

Levain Bakery

167 W 74TH ST, NEW YORK (UWS); 2167 FREDERICK
DOUGLASS BLVD, NEW YORK (HARLEM).

In a city with killer cookies at every turn, Levain Bakery could take the crown. The mega cookies eschew traditional width for height (more dome than disc) and weigh in at 180 g (6½ oz) each. It's a tough pick between the chocolate chip walnut, dark chocolate chocolate chip, dark chocolate peanut butter, and oatmeal and raisin, which is why you should get them all, like I do.

Mah-Ze-Dahr

28 GREENWICH AVE, NEW YORK (WEST VILLAGE).

It opened a week after I left (trust), so I can't personally vouch for it, but all reviews have been glowing for the brick-and-mortar shop of beloved baker and former wholesaler Umber Ahmad. Black and white cookies, brown butter blondies and brioche doughnuts are among the delicious selection.

Maman

211 W BROADWAY, NEW YORK (TRIBECA);
PLUS THREE MORE LOCATIONS.

You'll find French and American classics at this charming cafe–bakery, from viennoiserie and tarts to brownie jars and a chocolate chunk cookie studded with macadamias, walnuts and almonds. Their homemade Oreo gives Bouchon's TKO a run for its money, and the white chocolate and pretzel cookie is another knockout.

Momofuku Milk Bar

251 E 13TH ST, NEW YORK (EAST VILLAGE);
PLUS SIX MORE LOCATIONS.

The uber-cool dessert joint is known for many things (see *Pies*, page 145 and *Ice cream*, page 186), but I can't go past the b'day cake truffles and compost cookies packed with pretzels, potato chips and more. The inventive sweets, which cleverly repurpose leftovers and junk items, are the work of pastry chef Christina Tosi, who is as loved as her cult creations.

One Girl Cookies

68 DEAN ST, BROOKLYN (COBBLE HILL);
33 MAIN ST, BROOKLYN (DUMBO).

Whoopie pie is the signature here, but I come for the short, buttery cookies, delicate cupcakes and lemon-flecked scones, too. It's a neighbourhood favourite, and a sweet place to relax, sip tea and linger.

Ovenly

31 GREENPOINT AVE, BROOKLYN (GREENPOINT).

Vegan salted choc chip and gluten-free peanut butter masquerading as regular cookies are among the rustic baked goods that make this sweet bakery a Brooklyn darling. So are the elegant layer cakes (see *Cakes*, page 145), chocolate brownies heightened with black cocoa and, my pick, seasonal scones in sweet and savoury combos such as rosemary-currant and blackberry-mint.

Schmackary's

362 W 45TH ST, NEW YORK (HELL'S KITCHEN).

A locals' favourite, Schmackary's is all about big, warm, freshly baked cookies. Chocolate chip and funfetti are the crowd pleasers, but changing flavours range from red velvet with cream cheese to maple-bacon and matcha. Don't go past the best snickerdoodle in town with generous swirls of cinnamon sugar.

Sullivan Street Bakery

533 W 47TH ST, NEW YORK (HELL'S KITCHEN);
236 9TH AVE, NEW YORK (CHELSEA).

Could this be the best bombolini ever? Yes. It could also be the best doughnut in NYC. Made with panettone dough, filled with delicate vanilla custard and dusted with icing sugar, Jim Lahey's petite rounds are as light as air and absolutely ethereal. Home to some of the city's best artisan bread, too.

The City Bakery

3 W 18TH ST, NEW YORK (FLATIRON).

The pretzel croissant and hot chocolate may be its most Instagrammed items (see *Pastries*, page 103 and *Drinks*, page 187), but The City Bakery's chocolate chip cookie, peanut butter sandie and blueberry corn muffin are also taste sensations. In fact, you could pick almost anything here and, guaranteed, you'd swoon.

OTHER NOTABLES: Amy's Bread, Fat Witch Bakery, Jacques Torres Chocolate.

Restaurants

Manila Social Club

2 HOPE ST, BROOKLYN (WILLIAMSBURG).

You'll need a lot of dough (excuse the pun) to get your hands on this doughnut. The hip Filipino restaurant begins with an ube (purple yam) base, adds Cristal champagne gel and frosting, then adds a final touch of bling with 24K pure gold leaf to garnish. It costs, unsurprisingly, $100 a pop, but you can nab a plain ube for just $3.50.

Pies 'n' Thighs

166 S 4TH ST, BROOKLYN (WILLIAMSBURG).

Channeling Southern flavours (fried chicken, waffles, biscuits), this popular brunch spot is also famed for its oversized cake doughnuts (flavours change daily), as well as the sourdough, which blurs the textural line between cake and yeasted varieties, and is the only one of its kind in the city. Available takeaway, too.

Rider

80 N 6TH ST, BROOKLYN (WILLIAMSBURG).

I love this cool joint, from the service to the fitout, and especially their doughnuts. They're fried to order, so are warm on arrival and chewy and soft and delicious. They're tossed in fennel seed sugar and served with crème fraîche, so they're a little bit special, too.

Untitled (at the Whitney Museum)

99 GANSEVOORT ST, NEW YORK (CHELSEA).

Cookies are no longer the reserve of bakeries and coffee shops. Now, they're cropping up in fine diners, including the restaurant at the Whitney Museum of American Art. Their big triple choc round is baked to order so they're perfectly gooey, and served with a glass of milk infused with Madagascan bourbon vanilla.

Pastries, buns & bites

Living the dream

DAY 20, DESSERT 82: NUTELLA PAIN AU
CHOCOLAT, ÉPICERIE BOULUD, UWS

'You *gotta* try the Nutella pain au chocolat,' a guy leaned over and said, noting my indecision (which was actually about how many to buy, *not* which one, but how was he to know I was a glutton on a mission?). My daughter and I were at Épicerie Boulud, as in French chef Daniel Boulud's sweet joint, for another girls' dessert date (just living the dream). And there's this classic from the French canon, in a traditional patisserie, souped up with hazelnut spread.

In New York, Jewish delis, Greek coffee shops, Korean-run grocery stores and Latino bodegas all signal a multicultural city whose rich heritage and minority-majority makeup is proudly woven through daily life, and also its delicious sweets.

Pastries, buns, breads and bites best showcase these kaleidoscopic ethnic influences: Italian cannoli, Eastern European rugelach, Chinese milk buns and more. And you can find them in new-age bakeries, mod patisseries and hip restaurants as well as their traditional homes.

I'm partial to a classic (I'm talking to you, perfect sticky buns), but away from the homeland, unfettered by tradition or inspired by diversity, Gotham's pastry chefs are also experimenting with wild abandon and I relished the flavours of freedom: croissants twisted into pretzels, babka reimagined as doughnuts, matcha spilling out of chocolate moelleux, and cream puffs filled with black sesame cream, to name just a few.

'I get one every time I walk past, and I live around the corner,' he added, tucking into his bounty before he was even out the door. I guess he's living the NYC dream, too.

« *My indecision was actually about how many to buy, not which one, but how was he to know I was a glutton on a mission?* »

Whisky walnut babka

I first heard of this Eastern European pastry back in the 1990s. In more recent years, it taunted me on social media. I could bear it no more. And so it was that on the first afternoon of my sweet eating adventure, I went to Breads Bakery, ordered their legendary Nutella babka, and ate the whole thing.

The rich buttery brioche slathered in chocolate-hazelnut spread, rolled up, braided and drenched in sugar syrup is everything it promises. Bread's Nutella take also ignited a New York babka renaissance and now you can savour it as an ice-cream sandwich at Russ & Daughters, as a doughnut-babka hybrid at Dough, and more.

My babka takes inspiration from Arcade Bakery, another game-changer, where traditional brioche is replaced with laminated brioche for countless more soft flaky layers, and chocolate with boozy nuts. Like many pastries, there's time and work involved, but for me, this is the ultimate babka and worth every rest and fold. You'll also learn some neat new skills if you haven't tried your hand at laminating brioche before.

Combine the milk and yeast in a bowl and set aside for 5 minutes or until frothy, then whisk in the eggs. Using an electric mixer fitted with the dough hook, knead the flour, sugar, salt and yeast mixture until combined, then knead for a further 3 minutes. Add the butter, one piece at a time, mixing until incorporated before adding the next, then knead for a further 8 minutes or until smooth and elastic (the dough will be quite sticky). Shape into a ball and transfer to an oiled bowl. Cover loosely with plastic wrap, then set aside in a warm, draught-free place for 2 hours or until the dough has almost doubled in size.

Just before the dough has finished proving, set the extra 90 g (3 oz) butter aside at room temperature until it is just soft enough to roll (the goal is to have the dough and butter at roughly the same temperature). Place the butter between two sheets of baking paper and, using a rolling pin, roll out to a 12 cm (4¾ in) square.

Turn out the dough onto a lightly floured work surface and roll out to an 18 cm (7 in) square. Place the butter in the centre of the dough on the diagonal, so the corners are just touching the edges. Gently pull one corner of dough to stretch slightly, then fold it over the butter so it reaches the centre of the butter. Repeat with the remaining corners, then press the edges together to seal in the butter completely (make sure there are no gaps so the butter doesn't escape). Wrap the dough parcel in plastic wrap and refrigerate for 30 minutes or until the dough starts to firm up.

Place the dough parcel on a lightly floured work surface and, using a rolling pin, firmly press the dough at two ends to elongate slightly, then roll out to a 40 cm (16 in) × 12 cm (4¾ in) rectangle, ensuring the edges are straight and gently reshaping the corners into a square with your hands if necessary. Brush off any excess flour. With the short edge parallel to the work surface, fold the bottom third up, then the top third down over the bottom third, as you would a letter. Cover and refrigerate for 30 minutes or until the dough starts to firm up.

MAKES 2

60 ml (2 fl oz/¼ cup) lukewarm milk

1½ teaspoons dried yeast

2 eggs

260 g (9 oz/1¾ cups) plain (all-purpose) flour

2 tablespoons caster (superfine) sugar

1 teaspoon fine salt

110 g (4 oz) unsalted butter, cut into 2 cm (¾ in) pieces, softened, plus an extra 90 g (3 oz) cold butter, to laminate

recipe continued »

Rotate the dough parcel 90 degrees, then roll out to a 40 cm (16 in) × 12 cm (4¾ in) rectangle. Fold it into thirds like a letter (as before), then cover and refrigerate for 30 minutes or until it starts to firm up. Rotate the dough another 90 degrees, and repeat the rolling and folding. Cover and refrigerate for 30 minutes or until the dough starts to firm up.

Meanwhile, to make the filling, whisk the sugar and butter in a bowl to combine. Whisk in the flour and then the whisky, then set aside until needed. (If the mixture stiffens, warm it slightly just before using.)

Grease two 22 cm (8¾ in) × 11 cm (4¼ in) loaf tins. Divide the dough in half and refrigerate one portion until needed. Roll out the remaining dough on a lightly floured work surface to a 30 cm (12 in) × 22 cm (8¾ in) rectangle. Spread half the filling over the dough all the way to edges, then scatter over half the walnuts. Working from one long end, roll up the dough, pressing the edge to seal. Using a large sharp knife, cut lengthways through the centre of the dough. Place the pieces next to each other, cut side up. Starting from the top, braid the pieces, cut side up, then press the top and bottom edges together to seal slightly. Carefully transfer the babka to one of the prepared tins. Repeat with the remaining dough and filling, and place in the remaining tin. Loosely cover both tins with plastic wrap and set aside for 1½ hours or until risen.

Meanwhile, to make the glaze, combine the sugar and water in a small saucepan over medium–high heat and bring to the boil, stirring to dissolve the sugar. Cook for 1 minute, then remove from the heat and set aside until needed.

Preheat the oven to 190°C (375°F).

Bake the babkas, loosely covering with a sheet of foil halfway through to prevent overbrowning, for 28–30 minutes or until golden and cooked through. Remove from the oven and immediately brush over the glaze. Cool the babka in the tins for 5 minutes then, before the caramel hardens, turn out onto a wire rack to cool completely. Cut into slices to serve.

WHISKY WALNUT FILLING

220 g (8 oz/1 cup firmly packed) light brown sugar

80 g (2¾ oz) unsalted butter, melted

50 g (1¾ oz/⅓ cup) plain (all-purpose) flour

2 tablespoons scotch whisky

100 g (3½ oz/1 cup) walnuts, toasted, roughly chopped (or walnut pieces)

SUGAR SYRUP GLAZE

75 g (2¾ oz/⅓ cup) caster (superfine) sugar

60 ml (2 fl oz/¼ cup) water

TIP *The aim with laminated dough is to keep the butter encased in the dough at all times, so if butter is starting to melt or seep out, refrigerate the dough further. If the butter or dough is too stiff, rest it at room temperature for 5–10 minutes; this will make it easier to roll. If a little butter does break through, dust it lightly with flour to help mend the hole. And don't be daunted by the process – it's actually a lot of fun!*

WEST VILLAGE

17.19

East Village

A personal favourite and why I lived nearby. It's very real, and interesting at every turn.

No Relations Vintage has the best clothes. And cheap, too. Plus there's plenty of inspiration from locals on how to rock them.

I don't know why there are so many ice-cream shops in East Village, but I'm really happy about it. That and Momofuku Milk Bar and Veniero's are local, too.

Union Square Greenmarket

'Have you been to Union Square Greenmarket?' a local once asked me. 'It's the heartbeat of the city and a New York thing to do.' Yes, I had, and I just loved the description. Four days a week, summer through winter and rain, hail or shine, local farmers sell their bounty. The city's greenmarkets have been running for over four decades now and smaller sites bustle across the five boroughs, too. You can find the timetable at grownyc.org/greenmarket.

Sticky buns

In my opinion, sticky buns are up there with almond croissants and kouign amann as The Universe's Best Pastries. And it turns out the superlative versions are found in NYC, where they come in equal parts comfort food and elegant restraint.

At hip East Williamsburg pizzeria Roberta's, their cult bun is finished with sea salt flakes to temper the sticky buttery glaze, while at Sadelle's, the slick Jewish deli/ restaurant/bakery, the brown sugar topping permeates the bun and forms a crisp, candy-like shell.

These sticky buns are just as smart: flaky like a croissant, soft like brioche and with the perfect hit of brown sugar, cinnamon and butter. They're at their best still warm from the oven (or within a few hours), when I could almost eat the whole lot.

Combine the milk and yeast in a bowl and set aside for 5 minutes or until frothy, then whisk in the eggs. Using an electric mixer fitted with the dough hook, knead the flour, sugar, salt and yeast mixture until combined, then knead for a further 5 minutes. Add the butter, one piece at a time, mixing until incorporated before adding the next, then knead for a further 8 minutes or until smooth and elastic (the dough will be very sticky). Shape into a ball and transfer to a large oiled bowl. Cover loosely with plastic wrap, then set aside in a warm, draught-free place for 1 hour or until doubled in size.

Meanwhile, to make the cinnamon sugar, combine the cinnamon and sugar in a bowl.

To make the brown sugar glaze, using an electric mixer, beat the butter and sugar for 1 minute or until light and creamy.

Grease two 20 cm (8 in) square cake tins and line with foil, allowing plenty of overhang, then grease the foil. Spread the glaze mixture over the base of the tins and refrigerate until needed.

Knock back the dough, then divide in half. Working with one portion at a time, roll out on a lightly floured work surface to a 35 cm (14 in) × 30 cm (12 in) rectangle, with the longest edge parallel to the work surface. Using a pastry brush, brush the dough with water to moisten it slightly, then scatter over half the cinnamon sugar. Roll up the dough as tightly as you can, then press on the work surface to seal. Using a serrated knife, trim the ends, then cut the log into nine 3.5 cm (1½ in) thick pieces. Transfer to one of the prepared tins, cut side up, separating the pieces so they are evenly spaced (they will expand). Repeat with the remaining dough and cinnamon sugar and place in the remaining tin, then loosely cover the tins with oiled plastic wrap and set aside in a warm place for 1½ hours or until risen (there will still be space between the buns).

Preheat the oven to 180°C (350°F).

Loosely cover the tins with a sheet of foil to prevent overbrowning and bake, swapping the tins halfway through, for 40–45 minutes or until the buns are light golden on top. Remove from the oven and immediately invert onto a serving plate before the caramel hardens to reveal the sticky brown sugar glaze (take care as it's hot). Cool for 15 minutes, then sprinkle with sea salt flakes and serve warm or at room temperature.

MAKES 18

90 ml (3 fl oz) lukewarm milk

2 teaspoons dried yeast

3 eggs

350 g (12½ oz/2⅓ cups) plain (all-purpose) flour

2 tablespoons caster (superfine) sugar

1½ teaspoons fine salt

160 g (5½ oz) unsalted butter, cut into 2 cm (¾ in) pieces, softened

sea salt flakes, to sprinkle

CINNAMON SUGAR FILLING

2 teaspoons ground cinnamon

2 tablespoons caster (superfine) sugar

BROWN SUGAR GLAZE

250 g (9 oz) unsalted butter, chopped, softened

220 g (8 oz/1 cup firmly packed) light brown sugar

The restaurant–bakery

Sadelle's in Soho is so hot right now. It's a restaurant-meets-bakery and modern Jewish deli, two pretty big trends. On my first visit I ordered a sticky bun to take away. It was so good I came back for a sit-down meal and three-cheese blintze spilling with raspberry compote for dessert. The retro lab coat uniforms are a great touch.

Lafayette's chocolate coconut banana croissants

I didn't think you could improve on the almond croissant. Then I met the 'croissant du jour' at Lafayette Grand Café & Bakery and wondered why someone hadn't done a remake sooner. In place of almond meal was coconut frangipane. And instead of day-old croissants were pains au chocolat. The final touch: rounds of soft-baked banana and crisp coconut chips on top.

The French-American hybrid was *so* delectable that I asked patissier Jennifer Yee for the recipe – and she kindly obliged. Since then, I've been making these on repeat at my place. I just can't say no when faced with a good almond croissant, and this version, incredibly, is even better.

To make the pastry cream, pour the milk into a saucepan and bring almost to the boil over medium heat. Meanwhile, whisk the sugar and egg yolks until well combined, then add the cornflour and whisk to combine. Whisking constantly, gradually add the hot milk mixture until combined. Return the mixture to the saucepan and cook, whisking, over medium heat for 5 minutes or until thickened. Bring to a simmer and whisk for a further 3 minutes or until thick and glossy. Transfer to a bowl, then cover the surface with plastic wrap and refrigerate for 1 hour or until cold.

Preheat the oven to 180°C (350°F) and line two baking trays with baking paper.

To make the frangipane, using an electric mixer, beat the butter and icing sugar for 3 minutes until light and creamy. Add the pastry cream and beat until combined. Add the eggs, one at a time, beating until well combined after each addition. Combine the coconut and cornflour in a separate bowl, then add to the butter mixture, in three batches, beating until well combined. Set aside.

To make the syrup, place the sugar and water in a saucepan and bring to the boil over high heat, stirring to dissolve the sugar. Remove from the heat and stir in the rum. Keep the syrup warm.

Cut the pains au chocolat in half horizontally almost to the edge, leaving a hinge to open and close. Open the pains au chocolat and place, cut side up, on the prepared trays and brush all over with the warm rum syrup. Spread ¼ cup frangipane on the bottom half of each pain au chocolat, then top with three or four banana rounds. Close the pain au chocolat and brush the top with the remaining warm syrup, then spread the remaining frangipane over the top. Top with more banana rounds and scatter generously with coconut chips.

Bake, swapping the trays halfway through, for 25 minutes or until golden. Cool slightly on the trays, then dust with icing sugar to serve.

JENNIFER'S TIP *Assemble the pastries the night before and refrigerate until needed – they're great served for brunch. You'll just need to bake them for a little longer because they're going into the oven cold.*

MAKES 10

10 pains au chocolat

3 bananas, cut into 5 mm (¼ in) thick rounds

100 g (3½ oz) unsweetened coconut chips

pure icing (confectioners') sugar, to dust

PASTRY CREAM

180 ml (6 fl oz/¾ cup) milk

75 g (2¾ oz/⅓ cup) caster (superfine) sugar

2 egg yolks

1 tablespoon cornflour (cornstarch)

COCONUT FRANGIPANE

220 g (8 oz) unsalted butter, chopped, softened

300 g (10½ oz/2 cups) pure icing (confectioners') sugar, sifted

3 eggs

300 g (10½ oz/3¾ cups) dessicated coconut

2 tablespoons cornflour (cornstarch)

RUM SYRUP

150 g (⅔ cup) caster (superfine) sugar

150 ml (5 fl oz) water

250 ml (8½ fl oz/1 cup) rum

Nutella rugelach

You see rugelach just about everywhere in NYC, piled high in bagel shop windows, packaged on supermarket counters, and, the best kind, made daily in the city's cool bakeries and slick Jewish delis. How had I never met this scrumptious bite-sized sweet before? I was hooked.

Rugelach, I've since learned, is an American adaptation of another Jewish favourite, kipfel. One is made from sour cream pastry and is cookie-like; the other is a pastry made from yeasted dough, and you can savour both delicious incarnations. Highlights include The City Bakery's crumbly rolls spilling over with honey walnuts, Russ & Daughters' jammy rounds with raspberry, cinnamon and sunflower seeds, and the legendary chocolate rugelach at Breads Bakery, made with soft babka dough and shaped like mini croissants.

These rugelach are made with flaky cream cheese pastry that's laminated with Nutella, another New York obsession. The result is even more layers of chocolate (*yes!*) and a beautiful striped look. And they're so moreish.

Using an electric mixer, beat the butter and cream cheese until smooth and well combined. Add the flour and salt, and beat on low speed until combined. Shape into a rough block, then wrap in plastic wrap and refrigerate for 30 minutes or until just firm.

Roll out the pastry between two sheets of baking paper to a 30 cm (12 in) × 15 cm (6 in) rectangle with a short edge parallel to the work surface. Spread half the Nutella over the pastry, leaving a 1 cm (½ in) border. Fold the bottom third up, then the top third down over the bottom third, as you would a letter. Using your fingers, press the dough to seal in the Nutella (for perfect layers, the goal is to prevent any Nutella seeping out the ends or breaking through the pastry; if a little does, don't worry too much). Wrap in plastic wrap and refrigerate for 30 minutes or until just firm.

Rotate the parcel 90 degrees so the seam is on the right, then roll it out to a 30 cm (12 in) × 15 cm (6 in) rectangle. Spread over the remaining Nutella, leaving a 1 cm (½ in) border, then fold up and seal the edges again. Wrap in plastic wrap and refrigerate for a further 30 minutes or until just firm.

Preheat the oven to 180°C (350°F) and line a baking tray with baking paper.

Roll out the pastry to a 30 cm (12 in) × 20 cm (8 in) rectangle, with a long edge parallel to the work surface. Using a ruler and a large sharp knife, cut the pastry in half lengthways. Place one rectangle in the fridge until needed. Using the ruler, mark 7 cm (2¾ in) intervals along the top length then, 3.5 cm (1½ in) in from the corner, 7 cm (2¾ in) intervals along the bottom length. Using the marks as guides, cut the dough into eight triangles.

Working with one triangle at a time, roll it from the base of the triangle into a croissant shape, sealing the pointy end underneath. Transfer to the prepared tray and brush with eggwash. Bake for 20 minutes or until golden. Meanwhile, repeat the cutting, rolling and baking process with the remaining pastry rectangle.

Cool, then serve the rugelach warm or at room temperature.

MAKES ABOUT 16

125 g (4½ oz) unsalted butter, chopped, softened
125 g (4½ oz) cream cheese, chopped, softened
150 g (5½ oz/1 cup) plain (all-purpose) flour
¼ teaspoon fine salt
250 g (9 oz/¾ cup) Nutella
1 egg, lightly beaten

Krista, estate sales

'They say a picture is worth a thousand words, but here are four: try New York
babka! I can't get enough of it, from the buttery flavour to the way you can pull apart
the soft flaky ribbons. It's even better when Nutella and chocolate are swirled in.'

Chinatown

*Chinatowns around the world share the wonderful quality of being the same:
bustling, cheap and food havens.*

*10Below Ice Cream has four locations, and copycat ice-cream roll shops have spread
like wildfire around the city, but the original in Chinatown plays the best music.*

*My family loves Asian food, so we were always eating in Chinatown.
Shanghai Asian Manor has hands down the best Chinese.*

The new-wave bakery

Breads Bakery's Nutella babka is legendary. The guys here turn out all
sorts of reimagined Jewish pastries, and top-notch cakes, tarts and cookies in
general. It's all about artisan ingredients and ancient techniques. You can also
grab savoury meals and sit down to eat – New York bakeries are like that –
and the place feels like a cool canteen for grown-ups.

Peanut butter & jelly cannoli

One of New York's mutual talents is a respect and disregard for tradition. Take cannoli. Adopted by New Yorkers as if their own, the sweet migrant classic is immortalised in the must-see gilded Italian bakeshops of yesteryear in Little Italy and beyond.

But it is also reworked in mod restaurants in bold new flavours, including Santina, where mini waffle batter tubes come with cherry, pistachio and coconut-enriched ricotta (loved this), and Quality Italian's pumpkin take, finished tableside on a cannoli cart (so fun).

Likewise, my cannoli, filled with luscious peanut butter mousse and sweet strawberry conserve, is the ultimate New York-Italian mash-up. A little bit old school, a little bit cool.

You will need cannoli moulds or cannelloni pasta tubes to shape the cannoli.

Sift the flour and cocoa into a bowl. Add the butter and, using your fingers, rub into the flour mixture until the mixture resembles breadcrumbs. Stir in the icing sugar and salt. Add the vinegar and water and stir to form a dough (add an extra 1–2 teaspoons water if necessary). Using your hands, knead for 2 minutes or until smooth, then wrap in plastic wrap and refrigerate for 1 hour.

To make the peanut butter mousse, place the sugar and water in a small saucepan over medium–high heat. Bring to the boil, stirring until the sugar dissolves, then cook, without stirring, for 7 minutes or until the syrup reaches 115°C (240°F). Meanwhile, using an electric mixer, whisk the egg and egg yolks for 5 minutes until pale and tripled in volume. Whisking constantly, gradually add the hot syrup until combined, then whisk for 3 minutes or until cool. Add the peanut butter and whisk until just combined. In a clean bowl, whisk the cream to stiff peaks, then fold into the peanut butter mixture. Transfer the mousse to a piping (icing) bag fitted with a 1 cm (½ in) plain nozzle, then freeze for 1 hour to firm.

Meanwhile, fill a deep-fryer or saucepan one-third full of canola oil and heat over medium heat to 160°C (320°F). Divide the dough into two portions, then work with one portion at a time (refrigerate the remaining dough until needed). On a lightly floured work surface, roll out the dough until 1 mm (1/16 in) thick (it should be so thin you can almost see through it). Using a 10 cm (4 in) round cutter, cut out five rounds. Alternatively, using a sharp knife, cut into 10 cm (4 in) squares. Working with one round or square at a time, wrap around a cannoli mould, brushing one edge with egg white (make sure the egg white doesn't touch the mould or the cannoli shells will be hard to remove), then press the edges to seal.

recipe continued »

MAKES 10

150 g (5½ oz/1 cup) plain (all-purpose) flour

2 teaspoons unsweetened (Dutch) cocoa powder

25 g (1 oz) unsalted butter, chopped, softened

2 tablespoons pure icing (confectioners') sugar, sifted

pinch of fine salt

1 teaspoon white vinegar

60 ml (2 fl oz/¼ cup) water

canola oil, to deep-fry

1 egg white, lightly beaten

strawberry preserve or jam, to fill

finely chopped toasted peanuts, to serve (optional)

PEANUT BUTTER MOUSSE

110 g (4 oz/½ cup) caster (superfine) sugar

80 ml (2½ fl oz/⅓ cup) water

1 egg

2 egg yolks

140 g (5 oz/½ cup) smooth peanut butter

125 ml (4 fl oz/½ cup) thickened (whipping) cream

Fry the cannoli on the moulds, in batches, for 2 minutes or until crisp and blistered. Drain on paper towel and set aside to cool completely. Repeat with the remaining dough. Carefully remove the cannoli shells from the moulds and store in an airtight container until needed.

Just before serving, using a teaspoon, spoon in a little jam, then pipe in some mousse. Scatter the ends with peanuts, if using, and serve immediately.

TIP *A good cannoli relies on a shatteringly crisp shell, so roll out the dough as thinly as possible (it should be almost translucent), return the oil to 160°C (320°F) between batches, and pipe 'à la minute' (to order) to prevent softening.*

Lower East Side

A big neighbourhood with a storied past. It's pretty trendy now, but not that long ago countless migrants lived here in abject poverty.

The Tenement Museum is a real gem for history buffs, and everyone likes the gift shop. I picked up the best books, cards and kids' toys.

Russ & Daughters Cafe has a different lunch and dinner dessert menu, so naturally I went twice. It's a very cool restaurant and the offshoot of a 150-year-old deli around the corner.

Cronut

*Dominique Ansel's croissant–doughnut hybrid. New York's
(and possibly the world's) most famous dessert.*

FLAKY CROISSANT LAYERS + PASTRY CREAM CORE + SUGAR DUSTING +
GLISTENING GLAZE + MONTHLY CHANGING FLAVOURS
(LIKE BLACK CHERRY & VALRHONA CHOCOLATE)

*Apparently it was a snack for staff and just another creation.
The universe had other ideas about it …*

Carrot cake macarons

By 2011, fervour for the French classic was reaching fever pitch in the city. 'Your slacker boyfriend gives you cupcakes; your lover gives you macarons,' *The New York Times* even wrote. Other trends have since snatched the top title, but New York's love for macarons endures.

As a devotee myself, I savoured the selection at foreign imports (Ladurée), French patissiers (Bouchon) and dedicated parlours (Bisous Ciao), and flavours ranging from the traditional (salted caramel) to local and seasonal (blood orange).

It being New York, I couldn't resist the big bold American flavours, from key lime pie to peanut butter and jelly, and this macaron follows in their exuberant footsteps. With cream cheese buttercream studded with walnuts, and meringue laced with autumn spices, it tastes just like a delicious carrot cake, only more elegant, as only a French macaron can do.

Process the almond meal and icing sugar in a food processor until finely ground. Sift into a large bowl with the spices.

Place the caster sugar and water in a saucepan over medium heat and stir until the sugar dissolves. Bring to the boil, then cook, without stirring, for 5 minutes or until the mixture reaches 115°C (240°F). Using an electric mixer, whisk 55 g (2 oz) of the egg whites until soft peaks form. When the syrup reaches 118°C (245°F), immediately pour the hot syrup in a thin steady stream down the side of bowl, with the motor of the electric mixer running. Whisk for a further 5 minutes or until cool.

Place the remaining 55 g (2 oz) of egg whites in a small bowl and whisk in the food colouring. Add the tinted egg whites to the almond mixture and stir until a paste forms. Add the meringue and fold in until just combined, then continue folding until the mixture resembles a loose cake batter and slowly falls off the spatula (take care not to overfold as the mixture can go from the right consistency to too runny very quickly).

Line two baking trays with baking paper. Transfer the mixture to a piping (icing) bag fitted with a 9 mm (½ in) plain nozzle. Holding the bag upright and 1.5 cm (½ in) from the tray, pipe straight down to form 4 cm (1½ in) rounds, 2 cm (¾ in) apart, making a quick quarter turn of the nozzle to finish piping each round. Set the macarons aside at room temperature for 30 minutes or until a skin forms on the surface (it should not be tacky when gently touched).

Preheat the oven to 160°C (320°F).

Cook the macarons, one tray at a time, for 15 minutes or until the tops are firm to the touch and the shells can be easily removed from the tray (the shells should not be coloured). Set aside to cool completely.

MAKES 25

150 g (5½ oz/1¼ cups) almond meal

150 g (5½ oz/1 cup) pure icing (confectioners') sugar

½ teaspoon ground cinnamon

¼ teaspoon freshly grated nutmeg

¼ teaspoon ground cloves

150 g (5½ oz/⅔ cup) caster (superfine) sugar

60 ml (2 fl oz/¼ cup) water

110 g (4 oz) egg whites (from about 3 eggs)

orange food colouring, to colour (see tip)

100 g (3½ oz/1 cup) walnuts, toasted

CREAM CHEESE BUTTERCREAM

110 g (4 oz/½ cup) caster (superfine) sugar

60 ml (2 fl oz/¼ cup) water

1 egg

2 egg yolks

200 g (7 oz) unsalted butter, chopped, softened

250 g (9 oz) cream cheese, chopped, softened

Meanwhile, to make the buttercream, place the sugar and water in a saucepan over medium heat and stir until the sugar dissolves. Bring to the boil, then cook, without stirring, for 5 minutes or until mixture reaches 115°C (240°F). Meanwhile, using an electric mixer, whisk the egg and egg yolks until thick and pale. When the syrup reaches 118°C (245°F), with the motor running, immediately pour the hot syrup in a thin steady stream down the side of the bowl, then whisk for 5 minutes or until completely cool. In a clean bowl, beat the butter until light and fluffy, then add the egg mixture and beat until smooth. Add the cream cheese and beat until well combined. Transfer to a piping bag fitted with a 9 mm (½ in) plain nozzle.

Pipe mounds of buttercream onto the flat side of half the shells. Top with the walnuts, then cover with a little more buttercream. Sandwich with the remaining macaron shells.

Refrigerate the macarons for 24 hours, then bring to room temperature just before serving. They will keep in an airtight container in the fridge for up to 1 week.

TIP *All food colouring is not created equal. Liquid colouring, from supermarkets, is the weakest (you'll need a lot for intense colour), while pastes and powdered dyes, from speciality suppliers, are the strongest (take care not to use too much). Gel, available in some supermarkets, sits in the middle. Colour also diminishes as you add additional ingredients. Basically, experiment and don't worry if you don't hit the desired colour on your first attempt.*

Enriched & laminated doughs with Roger Gural, Arcade Bakery

GOOD FAT

Use European-style cultured butter with 83% butter fat for the best flavour and finish.

KEEP COOL

Brioche is mixed intensively, so make sure the eggs, milk, butter and water are cold or the dough temperature may rise too high. Fat also inhibits the formation of gluten, so we add it towards the end of mixing after moderate gluten development has been achieved.

SWEET SPOT

For laminated doughs, such as our babka (we use a laminated brioche), fully ferment the dough before the butter 'lock-in'. This makes a big difference to the flavour. Meanwhile, butter should be as cold as possible but still pliable – it will bend to a 90-degree angle but not crack. We pound it with a rolling pin to soften.

Little Italy

In the late 1800s, Italian immigrants set up camp on this stretch of Manhattan. The area's much smaller now, but still feels like the homeland.

The street art is epic. My husband's favourite is Audrey Hepburn (above); mine is Temper Tot with pink and green creatures that look like Hulk's kids.

I like new-school cannoli more than Little Italy's traditional ones. When I'm in the area, I go to Maman for a cookie dough ice-cream sandwich instead.

Black sesame cream puffs

Classic French patisserie and American bakeshop goods reimagined with exotic Asian ingredients is having a moment in Gotham's sun: hojicha ice cream, green tea brownies, Mont Blanc infused with yuzu and more. I was in heaven.

The cream puff, with its plain choux base, is a constant source of inspiration for local chefs, and filled with everything from earl grey and matcha to my new love, black sesame (you could find all three at Bibble & Sip). The it ingredient has a nutty and sophisticated flavour and, when blended with pastry cream, turns a striking grey colour.

These puffs are slightly larger than run-of-the-mill American varieties and are topped with traditional sablé à choux or craquelin (a streusel-like mixture that adds sweetness and crunch, and gives the choux a uniform dome shape). For me, they're elegant yet edgy, and best enjoyed piped to order when the choux is still crisp.

To make the craquelin, using an electric mixer, beat the butter and sugar in a bowl until well combined. Add the flour and beat on low speed until just combined. Shape into a disc, wrap in plastic wrap and refrigerate for 1 hour or until firm.

Preheat the oven to 180°C (350°F) and line two baking trays with baking paper.

Place the milk, butter, sugar, salt and water in a saucepan over medium–high heat. Cook until the butter melts, then bring to the boil. Add the flour and beat constantly with a wooden spoon until the mixture thickens and pulls away from the side of the pan. Cook, stirring, for a further 1 minute to develop the gluten.

Transfer to the bowl of an electric mixer and beat for 1 minute to release most of the heat. Add the eggs, one at a time, beating until well combined after each addition, then beat for a further 1 minute or until glossy.

Transfer the choux dough to a piping (icing) bag fitted with a 1.5 cm (½ in) plain nozzle and pipe 5 cm (2 in) rounds onto the prepared trays. Roll out the craquelin between two sheets of baking paper until 3 mm (⅛ in) thick. Using a 4.5 cm (1¾ in) round cutter, cut out rounds and place on top of the choux. Scatter black sesame seeds generously over the craquelin. Bake, one tray at a time and covering with a sheet of foil for the last 10 minutes to prevent overbrowning, for 40 minutes or until puffed, golden and crisp (the choux pastry should feel hollow when lifted from the tray). Transfer to a wire rack to cool completely.

recipe continued »

MAKES 16

60 ml (2 fl oz/¼ cup) milk

125 g (4½ oz) unsalted butter, chopped

1 teaspoon caster (superfine) sugar

1 teaspoon fine salt

125 ml (4 fl oz/½ cup) water

150 g (5½ oz/1 cup) plain (all-purpose) flour

4 eggs

BLACK SESAME CRAQUELIN

110 g (4 oz) unsalted butter, chopped, softened

110 g (4 oz/½ cup) raw (demerara) sugar

110 g (4 oz/¾ cup) plain (all-purpose) flour

black sesame seeds, to scatter

Meanwhile, to make the black sesame pastry cream, pour the milk into a saucepan and bring almost to the boil over medium heat. Meanwhile, whisk the sugar, cornflour, eggs and egg yolk in a bowl until well combined and pale. Whisking constantly, gradually add the hot milk until combined. Return the mixture to the saucepan and cook, whisking, over medium heat for 5 minutes or until thickened. Bring to a simmer and whisk for a further 2 minutes or until thick and glossy. Transfer to a bowl, then cover the surface with plastic wrap and refrigerate for 1 hour or until cold.

Using an electric mixer, whisk the cream to stiff peaks. Fold the black sesame paste into the pastry cream until well combined, then fold in the whipped cream. Transfer the mixture to a piping bag fitted with a 3 mm (⅛ in) plain nozzle.

Just before serving, make a small hole in the base of each choux puff and pipe in the black sesame pastry cream, tapping the puff gently to make space for more cream (you may have some cream left over). Serve immediately or store in an airtight container in the fridge for up to 1 day.

BLACK SESAME PASTRY CREAM

500 ml (17 fl oz/2 cups) milk

220 g (8 oz/1 cup) caster (superfine) sugar

2 tablespoons cornflour (cornstarch)

2 eggs

1 egg yolk

250 ml (9 fl oz/1 cup) thickened (whipping) cream

75 g (2¾ oz/¼ cup) black sesame paste (see tip)

TIPS *Black sesame paste should be pure, so check the ingredients carefully (red beans and sugar are often misleadingly added). The best quality is available from Japanese grocers. You can also make the choux puffs ahead. Store them in an airtight container, then re-crisp in a 160°C (320°F) oven for 8 minutes. Cool completely, then pipe.*

NOHO
13.17

Concord grape & thyme foccacia

I had the extremely good fortune of living 10 minutes from Union Square Greenmarket, the city's beloved farmers' market that runs four days a week, year round, even in the depths of winter, which meant that every time I walked past, I'd grab something sweet to eat then, or bake with later. It was the best.

Come late summer, dark purple, floral-flavoured concord grapes (a native American grape species) are in abundance. New York chefs put them in all manner of desserts, from La Newyorkina's popsicles to Four & Twenty Blackbirds' pie, and locals go, well, bananas for them.

So I bought my first-ever bunch, plus fresh thyme, with plans for this rustic fruit foccacia, inspired by those I'd savoured at epicurean Italian food hall Eataly and Williamsburg hotspot Lilia. Somewhat savoury and just sweet, it's a gorgeous morning or afternoon snack that allows fine produce to shine.

Combine the yeast, sugar and water in the bowl of an electric mixer fitted with the dough hook and set aside for 5 minutes or until frothy. Add the flour, salt and olive oil, and knead for 10 minutes or until smooth and elastic (the dough will be very sticky). Shape into a ball and transfer to an oiled bowl. Cover loosely with plastic wrap, then set aside in a warm, draught-free place for 1 hour or until doubled in size.

Line a baking tray with baking paper. Using floured hands, knock back the dough and divide into two portions. On a lightly floured work surface, shape each portion into a 15 cm (6 in) round (don't worry if it's more oval, it's supposed to be rustic), then transfer to the prepared tray. Set aside in a warm, draught-free place for 45 minutes or until almost doubled in size.

Preheat the oven to 180°C (350°F).

Meanwhile, to make the topping, place the butter and sugar in a small saucepan over medium heat and cook, stirring occasionally, until the butter is melted (you don't want to dissolve the sugar as the crystals give a crunchy topping). Gently spread most of the sugar mixture evenly over the dough all the way to the edges, taking care not to deflate the dough. Press in the grapes and scatter over the thyme sprigs, then carefully spread over the remaining sugar mixture.

Bake for 22 minutes or until the top is golden and the bread is cooked through. Remove from the oven and cool slightly, then transfer to a wire rack to cool completely.

MAKES 2

2 teaspoons dried yeast
2 teaspoons caster (superfine) sugar
160 ml (5½ fl oz/⅔ cup) lukewarm water
225 g (8 oz/1½ cups) plain (all-purpose) flour
½ teaspoon fine salt
2 tablespoons extra-virgin olive oil

TOPPING
40 g (1½ oz) unsalted butter, chopped
55 g (2 oz/¼ cup) caster (superfine) sugar
1 bunch (150 g/5½ oz) concord or other black seedless grapes, grapes picked
10 small thyme sprigs

CENTRAL PARK
11.36

Hit list

Bakeries, patisseries & cafes

Arcade Bakery

220 CHURCH ST, NEW YORK (TRIBECA).

A New York highlight for every perfect pastry, and particularly babka. Available by the slice or whole in whisky pecan, chocolate walnut or poppy seed, it's everything wondrous about croissants and brioche in one. The small-batch bakery resides in an art deco building lobby, so the entrance and eating booths are really special, too.

Bibble & Sip

253 W 51ST ST, NEW YORK (MIDTOWN).

On top of some fine scones, this cute Asian-leaning cafe-patisserie has a local following for its picture-perfect cream puffs with creamy centres of earl grey, chocolate and matcha, and the moreish PB&J milk bun with condensed milk. The signature matcha jasmine latte is often adorned with kitty cat latte art for even more Instagram opportunities.

Bien Cuit

120 SMITH ST, BROOKLYN (BOERUM HILL).

This Scandi-styled artisan bakery in cool Boerum Hill is a hit for its viennoiserie, including the signature twice-baked almond croissant and tebirke, a sweet-savoury Danish with marzipan and poppy seeds. There's also seasonal Danish (think grape and bergamot) and jewel-like eclairs.

Breads Bakery

18 E 16TH ST, NEW YORK (FLATIRON);
1890 BROADWAY, NEW YORK (UWS).

If time's short, put this bakery on your must-try list. The babka, decadently swirled with Nutella and studded with dark chocolate chunks, has become a sweet New York icon. Meanwhile, its take on rugelach, made with babka dough and layered with chocolate or marzipan, is just as outrageous. (See also *Cookies*, page 59.)

Burrow

68 JAY ST, BROOKLYN (DUMBO).

Kouign amann is increasingly cropping up around town, and Burrow's version – buttery, sugary, custardy – is up there with the best. The secret Dumbo spot with French and Japanese tendencies also excels in cookies, including super-cute sugar varieties (see *Cookies*, page 59; and fawn over their Insta feed as I do) and sells Kettl tea, i.e. the best sencha you will ever try.

Cha-An Tea House

230 E 9TH ST, NEW YORK (EAST VILLAGE).

Head here for a little zen from the busy city and elegant Asian sweets that range from traditional to experimental. There's hojicha anmitsu (green tea jelly with black syrup) and house-made mochi filled with earl grey chocolate, plus black sesame crème brûlée and even a matcha rice krispie ice-cream sandwich. I could sit there for hours, and did.

Dessert Club, ChikaLicious

204 E 10TH ST, NEW YORK (EAST VILLAGE).

Bring an appetite, or better yet a friend, to eat all the sweets this locals' fave in Little Tokyo knocks up. First, order the famed bun chika bun bun, a crunchy crazy creation of speculaas baked into a milk bun, followed by tiramisu mochi, Boston cream puff and a Nutella dough'ssant, their take on the cronut.

Dominique Ansel Bakery

189 SPRING ST, NEW YORK (SOHO).

The cult bakery needs little introduction, nor its legendary cronut, which changes flavour monthly. Around 500 are baked daily and often sell out by 9 am (pre-order two weeks ahead to avoid disappointment). Since you're braving the lines, sample every Ansel signature as I did, including the caramelised croissant glory that is Dominique's Kouign Amann (DKA). (See also *Created*, page 232.)

Épicerie Boulud

1900 BROADWAY, NEW YORK (UWS);
PLUS TWO MORE LOCATIONS.

The patisserie-meets-providore of acclaimed French chef Daniel Boulud turns out impeccable viennoiserie. His signatures – the striped raspberry and white chocolate ganache croissant, and Nutella pain au chocolat – also come with a dash of American gusto and are as exquisite to look at as they are to eat.

Lafayette Grand Cafe & Bakery

380 LAFAYETTE ST, NEW YORK (NOHO).

Thankfully, dining at the adjoining restaurant isn't the only way to experience Lafayette's sweet offerings. The bakery upfront sells French viennoiserie, plus American cookies and bars, but the 'croissant du jour' steals the show. The bold take on almond croissant with banana, coconut and chocolate was so delicious I had to get the recipe – see page 76.

Seed + Mill

CHELSEA MARKET, 409 W 15TH ST, NEW YORK (CHELSEA).

Halva, the Middle East's sesame seed equivalent of nougat, is more tempting than ever at this gorgeous artisan producer in Chelsea Market. Giant mounds in around thirty flavours, from pistachio to white chocolate and lemon, are sliced to order, while the signature soft serve with tahini and goat's milk has haunted me since I tried it (in a good way!).

The City Bakery

3 W 18TH ST, NEW YORK (FLATIRON).

Chewy, flaky, soft, salty, buttery and doused in signature rock salt and sesame seeds, the pretzel croissant is infamous for a thousand good reasons. It's also the perfect accompaniment to another of master baker Maury Rubin's killer creations: The City Bakery hot chocolate (see *Drinks*, page 187).

Union Fare

7 E 17TH ST, NEW YORK (UNION SQUARE).

Croissants in wild flavours was the next trend exploding while I was in town. And while not all social media stars are worthy of the attention, these guys merit every second of it. It's the brainchild of pastry pro Thiago Silva, found at hot new gastro-hall Union Fare, and comes in birthday cake, red velvet, matcha and my pick, crème brûlée.

Diners & restaurants

High Street on Hudson

637 HUDSON ST, NEW YORK (WEST VILLAGE).

Another chic bakery-meets-restaurant, this relative newcomer has been a hit for its pastry selection. The range – from honey cake and chocolate brioche to snickerdoodles and peaches and cream Danish – runs out quick, so arrive early.

Locanda Verde

377 GREENWICH ST, NEW YORK (TRIBECA).

I can only speak for the coffee counter stocked with regional Italian pastries at this Tribeca hotspot, but if the fig jam shortbread is anything to go by, the rhubarb crostata, olive oil semifreddo and almond tortino I spied on the dessert menu would be rustic deliciousness, too.

Quality Eats

19 GREENWICH AVE, NEW YORK (WEST VILLAGE).

Sensational monkey bread, warm from the oven and portioned to feed the whole table, and the black and white French toast doused with chocolate and vanilla creams, are reasons to come for brunch; the epic sundaes are reason to return for dessert (see *Ice Cream*, page 187).

Roberta's

261 MOORE ST, BROOKLYN (BUSHWICK).

Order it with brunch, have one for dessert alongside housemade gelati, or grab one to take away from the bakery next door. Just make sure you try the original hipster Bushwick pizza joint's signature sticky bun. Crunchy on the edges, giving in the centre, and scattered with sea salt flakes, it could be the best you've ever tried (I went back for thirds).

Sadelle's

463 W BROADWAY, NEW YORK (SOHO).

Dubbed the bagel whisperer, Melissa Welles' pastry case at this hip restaurant-bakery also features sweets baked into submission. The signature sticky bun, with wafer-thin layers of laminated dough and hard-glazed with brown sugar, is crisp, almost candy-like, and a taste sensation. The dine-in cheese blintze is also excellent.

Santina

820 WASHINGTON ST, NEW YORK (CHELSEA).

Cannoli is given a makeover at this pumping brunch spot under the High Line. Tubes made from waffle batter are even better than the original, while ricotta fillings come in three delectable flavours: pistachio, cherry and, my fave, coconut. I almost ordered another serve. The lime meringa is another hit.

Cakes, pies & puddings

The weekend's here

DAY 39, DESSERT 161: BOURBON GINGER
PECAN PIE, BUTTER & SCOTCH, CROWN HEIGHTS

Imagine this: it's 11 am on a Saturday and we're at a bakery-meets-bar called Butter & Scotch, which means I'm eating a slab of bourbon ginger pecan pie and my husband's downing a seriously boozy milkshake. This is actually a thing here! My mind is exploding (and I'm not even the drunk one).

They call it brunch, the New York weekend tradition of food, a group of friends and bottomless drinks that runs until dinner. At Butter & Scotch, they've adroitly added dessert to the mix.

These days, as nostalgia takes centre stage, you can savour Americana favourites – layered cakes, rustic pies and custard puddings – just about everywhere, from pie shops and bakeries to chic salons, cool restaurants, fine diners and, it seems, even bars.

The selection is marked by seasonal flavours (and it's a city where seasons are clearly delineated, unlike in Sydney, where I'm from) and the produce on display at the greenmarket – a light buttermilk custard with peach and basil in summer, a late springtime matcha cake with strawberries, pumpkin pies in autumn, and chess pies come winter. Just don't mess with New York all-time favourites apple pie, blackout cake, birthday cake and cheesecake; they could never be dropped from menus even if someone was foolish enough to try.

On Sunday, we set out for Four & Twenty Blackbirds, another incredible Brooklyn pie joint in Gowanus. There was no boozing there, but the scene was just to my liking: cups of coffee and tea, parents with kids, heads buried in newspapers and everyone eating big wedges of pie covered with whipped cream. *It was 8 am.* Gosh, I love this city.

When two encounters with pie can sum up a sweet New York weekend …

« *It's 11 am on a Saturday and we're at a bakery-meets-bar called Butter & Scotch, which means I'm eating a slab of bourbon ginger pecan pie and my husband's downing a seriously boozy milkshake.* »

Peaches & cream cupcakes

No conversation about New York sweets is complete without cupcakes. The pretty little frosting-topped rounds ignited a worldwide obsession that still burns today, years after Magnolia Bakery appeared in an episode of *Sex and The City* (widely agreed to be ground zero for the epidemic).

Before my trip I didn't really see the fuss (sorry cupcake lovers), but boy did I meet some compelling varieties at Molly's Cupcakes and Sweet Revenge: rustic, inventive and bursting with flavour. Magnolia's famous red velvet is up there with them, too.

Likewise, these cupcakes will enchant every type of sweet tooth with their dreamy mix of vanilla almond cake, peach curd core and crème fraîche whipped cream topping. They're soft, light, buttery and delectable, and taste just like summer.

To make the peach curd, process the peach flesh in a food processor until very smooth. Transfer 250 ml (8½ fl oz/1 cup) to a saucepan with the lemon juice, sugar and egg yolks, and whisk to combine. Place the pan over medium heat and cook, whisking, for 20 minutes or until thickened. Remove from the heat and whisk in the butter until melted and combined. Transfer to a bowl, cover the surface with plastic wrap and refrigerate for 2 hours or until cold and set.

Meanwhile, preheat the oven to 180°C (350°F) and line twelve 80 ml (2½ fl oz/ ⅓ cup) holes of a cupcake tin with paper cases.

Sift the flour, almond meal, baking powder and salt into a bowl and set aside. Using an electric mixer, beat the butter and sugar until light and creamy. Add the eggs, one at a time, beating well after each addition, then beat in the vanilla. In batches, alternately add the flour mixture and milk, beating until well combined. Fill the cupcake papers three-quarters full, then bake for 20 minutes or until the centre springs back when gently touched. Cool in the tin for 5 minutes, then transfer the cupcakes to a wire rack to cool completely.

To make the crème fraîche cream, using an electric mixer, whisk the cream, crème fraîche and icing sugar to stiff peaks. Refrigerate until needed.

To assemble, cut each peach into six wedges, then gently toss with the rosewater in a bowl, if using. Alternatively, place in a bowl of acidulated water (add a little bit of lemon or lime juice to water) to prevent browning. Using a small sharp knife, cut out a 3.5 cm (1½ in) diameter cone from the centre of each cupcake, taking care not to go through the base (the cones are now yours to snack on). Fill the centres with peach curd, then top each cupcake with a rough quenelle of cream and a peach wedge and serve.

MAKES 12

185 g (6½ oz/1¼ cups) plain (all-purpose) flour

30 g (1 oz/¼ cup) almond meal

1½ teaspoons baking powder

½ teaspoon fine salt

125 g (4½ oz) unsalted butter, chopped, softened

165 g (6 oz/¾ cup) caster (superfine) sugar

2 eggs

1 teaspoon natural vanilla extract

160 ml (5½ fl oz/⅔ cup) milk

2 white peaches (or nectarines)

1 tablespoon rosewater (optional)

WHITE PEACH CURD

4 (about 650 g/1 lb 7 oz) white peaches (or nectarines), peeled, stones removed

60 ml (2 fl oz/¼ cup) lemon juice

150 g (5½ oz/⅔ cup) caster (superfine) sugar

4 egg yolks

100 g (3½ oz) unsalted butter, chopped

CRÈME FRAÎCHE CREAM

330 ml (11 fl oz/1⅓ cups) thickened (whipping) cream

2 tablespoons crème fraîche (or sour cream)

75 g (2¾ oz/½ cup) icing (confectioners') sugar, sifted

New York cheesecake

I'd only known lofty, dense New York cheesecakes topped with a layer of sour cream. I didn't get the big deal. But a real New York cheesecake? Now that's a different thing altogether: smooth, creamy, just sweet, and decadent without feeling cloying. In other words: perfection.

There doesn't seem to be one definition for the style, but the best I read described it as 'unadulterated' – just cream cheese, cream (or sour cream), sugar and eggs. As with anything simple, the art is in the act of balance, each ingredient in just the right proportion, and fastidiousness when baking.

I don't think you've *really* tried a New York cheesecake until you've had one at Two Little Red Hens, Eileen's, Veniero's or, my favourite (just), recklessly covered with uber-thick whipped cream known as schlag at Peter Luger's – they all just nail it. I also read that New York cheesecake gets its name from the simple but all-defining fact it's made in New York. But this guy, it comes really close.

Position an oven rack in the lower third of the oven, then preheat the oven to 160°C (320°F). Wrap foil around the outside of a 23 cm (9 in) springform tin to prevent batter dripping out, then grease the tin and line the base with baking paper.

To make the crumb base, place the crackers or biscuits and sugar in a food processor and process until finely ground. Add the melted butter and process until well combined. Tip into the prepared tin and press until evenly spread and compact.

In a clean large food processor (or in batches if your processor isn't large enough), process the cream, sugar, eggs and vanilla for 1 minute or until combined. Add the cream cheese and process for 1 minute or until completely smooth, scraping down the sides of the bowl to remove any lumps. With the motor running, add the cooled melted butter and process until just combined. Pour into the tin, smooth the top, then gently tap the tin on a work surface to remove air bubbles. Tap again after 1 minute.

Bake the cheesecake for 45–50 minutes or until slightly risen and just set on top (it will wobble slightly if the tin is gently shaken or the top is gently touched). Remove from the oven and cool completely in the tin. Cover with plastic wrap and refrigerate for at least 4 hours or overnight until completely chilled.

Meanwhile, to make the whipped cream, using an electric mixer, whisk the cream, sugar and vanilla extract until soft peaks form.

Turn the cheesecake out onto a serving platter and bring to room temperature 20 minutes before serving. Cut into pieces and serve with the whipped cream.

TIPS *The key to a smooth, silky cheesecake without cracks is minimal air in the batter. Use a food processor, as it blends rather than whips, but only process until just combined. Mild heat and slow cooling are also critical, so monitor the temperature and follow the instructions in the recipe closely.*

SERVES 10–12

375 ml (12½ fl oz/1½ cups) pouring (whipping/heavy) cream

220 g (8 oz/1 cup) caster (superfine) sugar

4 eggs

1 tablespoon natural vanilla extract

1 kg (12 lb 3 oz) cream cheese, chopped, softened

80 g (2¾ oz) unsalted butter, melted, cooled

CRUMB BASE

200 g (7 oz) graham crackers or digestive biscuits

75 g (2¾ oz/⅓ cup) golden caster (superfine) sugar (or organic cane sugar)

125 g (4½ oz) unsalted butter, melted

WHIPPED CREAM

500 ml (17 fl oz/2 cups) thickened (whipping) cream

35 g (1¼ oz/¼ cup) icing (confectioners') sugar

1 teaspoon natural vanilla extract

A brief history of New York cheesecake

Few iconic New York dishes overshadow the cheesecake. The style now synonymous with the city made its first appearance in the early twentieth century, when a product called Philadelphia Cream Cheese (produced in New York State) came onto the market. Producers targeted Jewish restaurants, which turned it into the simple but creamy dessert. Turf Restaurant claims the original creation; it's no longer around, but Lindy's and Junior's are still going strong. Peter Luger Steakhouse, Eileen's and Two Little Red Hens are now famous for the cake, too.

Terry, creative director

'Eileen's was the first place I realised why New York is famous for cheesecake.'

Chelsea/Meatpacking

It's pretty cultured over here. In the 1990s, contemporary art galleries flooded the neighbourhood, but the area still feels welcoming and accessible.

How incredible is the High Line? Set in a disused aerial railroad, the park-cum-outdoor gallery epitomises New York's creative use of space and love for public art.

I'd like to make it up to The Standard's rooftop bar, but I keep getting distracted by desserts like green tea and mango bombe Alaska at the hotel's Standard Grill.

Brooklyn blackout cake

My first encounter with the Brooklyn blackout was ten years ago when I stumbled upon a recipe and was immediately taken with the mysterious name. Then I saw a picture of the deep dark beast. It looked like (*and was …*) the chocolate cake of my dreams.

Inspired by the blackout drills of World War II, when city lights were muted and windows covered with black, Brooklyn chain Ebinger's Bakery created the rich moist cake with chocolate pudding filling and glossy choc frosting. The bakery closed in 1972, but scores of New York bakeries continue the tradition, including the best classic take at Two Little Red Hens, Ovenly's mod pitch-black rendition, and an insane doughnut incarnation at Doughnut Plant.

My BB takes its cue from Christina Tosi's naked cakes, complete with layers of soaked chocolate-espresso cake, Oreo-laced buttercream, sticky chocolate fudge frosting and crunchy chocolate-coffee crumbs, in breathtaking shades of black and brown. It's a little (well, a lot) of work, but so was the original and it's worth every single bite.

Preheat the oven to 180°C (350°F). Wrap foil around the outside of two 20 cm (8 in) round springform cake tins to prevent any batter dripping out, then grease and line the bases with baking paper.

Sift the flour, cocoa, bicarbonate of soda, baking powder and salt into a large bowl. Using an electric mixer, beat the eggs and sugar for 2 minutes or until thick and pale. Add the oil and beat until well combined. In batches, alternately add the flour mixture and sour cream, beating on low speed until just combined. Add the coffee and vanilla, and stir well to combine (the batter will be quite runny).

Divide the batter evenly between the prepared tins, then bake for 45 minutes or until a skewer inserted into the centre of each cake comes out clean. Cool in the tins for 15 minutes, then turn out onto a wire rack to cool completely.

Reduce the oven temperature to 150°C (300°F).

Meanwhile, to make the chocolate-coffee crumbs, line a baking tray with baking paper. Sift the flour, cocoa, sugar, cornflour and salt into a bowl. Add the butter and coffee and, using an electric mixer, beat until the mixture comes together in small balls. Spread out on the prepared tray and bake for 20 minutes or until dry. Allow to cool completely, then loosely crumble and transfer to an airtight container until needed.

To make the Oreo buttercream, process the chocolate wafers in a food processor to fine crumbs (make sure there are no small chunks or the buttercream won't be smooth). Add the cream and melted butter and process until moistened and well combined. Add the milk and process until smooth. In a seperate, clean bowl, using an electric mixer, beat the icing sugar and the extra 200 g (7 oz) of butter for 3 minutes or until light and creamy. Then, add the chocolate mixture and beat for a further 2 minutes or until smooth. Set aside at room temperature until needed.

SERVES 16–20

250 g (9 oz/1⅔ cups) plain (all-purpose) flour

100 g (3½ oz/1 cup) unsweetened (Dutch) cocoa powder

2 teaspoons bicarbonate of soda (baking soda)

1 teaspoon baking powder

½ teaspoon fine salt

2 eggs

440 g (15½ oz/2 cups) caster (superfine) sugar

125 ml (4 fl oz/½ cup) canola oil

240 g (8½ oz/1 cup) sour cream

250 ml (8½ fl oz/1 cup) espresso or strong brewed coffee, at room temperature

1 teaspoon natural vanilla extract

milk, to brush

CHOCOLATE-COFFEE CRUMBS

50 g (1¾ oz/⅓ cup) plain
(all-purpose) flour

35 g (1¼ oz/⅓ cup) unsweetened
(Dutch) cocoa powder

55 g (2 oz/¼ cup) caster
(superfine) sugar

1 teaspoon cornflour (cornstarch)

½ teaspoon fine salt

50 g (1¾ oz) unsalted butter,
melted

2 teaspoon espresso or strong
brewed coffee, at room
temperature

OREO BUTTERCREAM

320 g (11½ oz) Nabisco Famous
Chocolate Wafers (see tip)

125 ml (4 fl oz/½ cup) pouring
(whipping/heavy) cream

50 g (1¾ oz) unsalted butter,
melted, plus an extra 200 g
(7 oz) unsalted butter,
chopped, softened

160 ml (5½ fl oz/⅔ cup) milk

75 g (2¾ oz/½ cup) pure icing
(confectioners') sugar, sifted

CHOCOLATE FUDGE FROSTING

50 g (1¾ oz) dark chocolate
(55% cocoa solids), finely
chopped

25 g (1 oz/¼ cup) unsweetened
(Dutch) cocoa powder

90 g (3 oz/¼ cup) glucose syrup

2 tablespoons caster (superfine)
sugar

80 ml (2½ fl oz/⅓ cup) pouring
(whipping/heavy) cream

To assemble the cake, using a large serrated knife, trim the tops off the cakes to make them level, then cut each cake in half horizontally. Place one base cake layer on a cake stand, then brush generously with milk. Spread over one-third of the buttercream all the way to the edges. Repeat this layering with two more cake layers, milk and buttercream. Finish with the remaining cake base, bottom side up, then brush generously with milk. Refrigerate for 30 minutes to firm slightly.

Meanwhile, to make the fudge frosting, place the chocolate and cocoa in a heatproof bowl. Place the remaining ingredients in a saucepan over medium heat and cook, stirring, until melted. Pour over the chocolate and cocoa, stand for 1 minute, then whisk until melted and smooth. Set aside to cool to a spreadable consistency.

Using a palette knife, carefully scrape and smear any buttercream around the side of the cake to smooth and achieve a 'naked' effect. Spread the fudge frosting over the top, then pile on the chocolate crumbs and serve.

TIP *If you can't find Nabisco Famous Chocolate Wafers, use Oreos with the vanilla filling scraped off. It's a little wasteful, but no other chocolate cookie matches the dark choc flavour of these guys. Alternatively, make another two batches of the chocolate crumbs, omitting the coffee, and use these in your buttercream instead of the wafers.*

The mod patisserie/cake salon

*At Lady M, every cake looks so perfect it's nearly impossible to pick just one.
So I used to order three, including the signature mille crêpes, plus a pot of green tea.
Even though it's always full, it's usually very quiet, as if everyone is in awe of the
selection or in raptures about what they're eating.*

Noho

Short for North of Houston Street, it's one of New York's smallest neighbourhoods, but a favourite. It's super artsy (Andy Warhol used to live here).

Lafayette Grand Cafe & Bakery feels like a slice of Paris in the Big Apple.

Right next to Bleecker Street Subway, there's the thinnest building I've ever seen (above). I used to spend minutes pondering its construction and purpose every time I walked past.

Butter & Scotch's birthday cake

If you didn't know that 'birthday cake' is a specific type of cake and not an all-encompassing term, you're not the only one. In New York, I was quick to find out. The much-loved layered cake, also known as funfetti, can now be found in every inspired shape and form, from cake truffles and cookies to sundaes and even croissants.

I became an immediate fan, particularly of the classic, where the delicious and good-looking combination of vanilla cake, buttery frosting and rainbow sprinkles really shines. In my opinion, the best birthday cake is found at Butter & Scotch, a bakery-bar where Allison Kave and Keavy Landreth pour a mean drink to go with the finest cake and pie.

This recipe is from their fantastic book, *Butter & Scotch: Recipes from Brooklyn's Favorite Bar and Bakery* (Abrams Books), and they kindly shared it with a tip: 'Serve with a crisp, dry cava or real-deal Champagne. It's a great foil to the sweet, creamy richness.' It is a birthday cake after all.

Preheat the oven to 175°C (350°F). Grease three 23 cm (9 in) round cake tins, then dust with flour, tapping out the excess.

Chop the butter into small, pea-sized pieces and return to the fridge. Bring the milk to room temperature by zapping it in a microwave for 30 seconds, then add the vanilla and set aside.

Using an electric mixer, beat the flour, baking powder, salt and 500 g (1 lb 2 oz) of the sugar on low speed for 30 seconds to combine. Add the cold butter, then increase the speed to medium and beat until the butter breaks down and the flour mixture is the texture of wet sand. Reduce the speed to low and beat in the milk mixture.

In a separate clean bowl, whisk the egg whites and remaining 300 g (10½ oz) of sugar on high speed until soft peaks form. Gently fold the meringue into the flour and milk mixture until well combined.

Divide the batter evenly among the prepared tins and bake, rotating halfway through, for 30–40 minutes or until golden and a skewer inserted into the centre comes out clean. Transfer the tins to a wire rack for 10 minutes before turning the cakes out of the tins to cool completely.

recipe continued »

SERVES 12–20

455 g (1 lb) cold unsalted butter

660 ml (22½ fl oz/2⅔ cups) milk

1½ tablespoons natural vanilla extract

500 g (1 lb 2 oz/3⅓ cups) plain (all-purpose) flour

50 g (1¾ oz) baking powder

2 teaspoons fine salt

800 g (1 lb 12 oz) caster (superfine) sugar

12 egg whites

Meanwhile, to make the frosting, using an electric mixer, beat the butter until smooth, making sure to stop the mixer every so often to scrape down the sides and bottom of the bowl (it's important the butter is nice and soft so you don't get any clumps of cold butter when piping the frosting). Add the cream cheese, one-quarter at a time, beating on medium speed until well combined. Beat in the vanilla and food colouring, then reduce the speed to low and gradually add the icing sugar. Crank up the speed to high and beat for 30 seconds or until well combined and fluffy.

Using a large serrated knife, trim the tops off the cakes to make them level. Frost and stack the three layers, then frost the sides. Decorate the sides with rainbow sprinkles.

VANILLA FROSTING

455 g (1 lb) unsalted butter, chopped, softened

455 g (1 lb) cream cheese, chopped, softened

1½ tablespoons natural vanilla extract

2–3 drops red food colouring

910 g (2 lb) pure icing (confectioners') sugar

rainbow sprinkles, to decorate

BUTTER & SCOTCH'S TIP *We decorate the top of our birthday cake with frosting rosettes, which you can do too by making another batch of vanilla frosting, putting it in a piping (icing) bag fitted with a 6 mm (¼ in) star nozzle and piping the rosettes around the edge.*

Greenwich Village

Home to NYU and lined with beautiful old brownstones, it feels like a picturesque university town, only better.

My favourite time to visit Washington Square Park (above) is twilight. Chess players take up residence, musicians harmonise and there's the most atmospheric light refracted off the arch.

Even at midnight, Mario Batali's OTTO Enoteca bustles with life, and the olive oil copetta tastes better every time we visit.

Banana cream mille crêpes

The French classic gâteau de crêpes (crêpe cake) has become one of the city's most sought-after desserts, thanks to Lady M, which evocatively dubbed (and later trademarked) theirs Mille Crêpes, a play on the famous mille feuille, and revived it in elegant new flavours: chocolate, citron, green tea, marron, earl grey and more.

The dessert can now be found at a host of sweet salons, but the chic Japanese-French patisserie's is a work of particular precision and refinement. I ordered a wedge of the original – twenty paper-thin crêpes layered with light pastry cream and a golden top à la brûlée – and sunk my fork in. It slid through the perfect tiers and the mouthful was délicatesse and flavour in one.

I've taken another NYC favourite – banana cream pie – as the backdrop for my own gâteau de crêpes, melding fresh banana, spiked Chantilly cream and little pops of graham cracker crumb. It's easier to make than its namesake, and just as special.

Blend the milk, eggs, butter, flour, caster sugar and salt until smooth, scraping down the sides to ensure there are no lumps. Set aside for 15 minutes for the bubbles to dissipate.

Heat a 20 cm (8 in) (base measurement) frying pan over medium heat. Lightly brush with extra melted butter, then pour 60 ml (2 fl oz/¼ cup) batter into the pan and swirl to evenly coat the base (reduce the heat slightly if the batter starts to set too quickly). Cook for 30–45 seconds or until just golden and cooked, then turn over and cook for a further 15 seconds or until just cooked. Transfer to a plate and repeat with the remaining batter to make about 15 crepes in all, brushing in between with a little melted butter. Stack the crêpes and set aside to cool.

To make the Graham cracker pie crumb, combine all the ingredients in a bowl, then spread over a baking paper-lined tray. Set aside for 20 minutes to firm, then crumble.

To make the cream for the filling, using an electric mixer, whisk the cream, condensed milk, icing sugar and vanilla in a bowl until stiff peaks form.

When you are ready to assemble, peel and very thinly slice the bananas. Place a crêpe in the centre of a serving plate and spread ⅓ cup filling almost to the edges. Scatter with one-third of the pie crumb and top with a crêpe. Spread over another ⅓ cup filling, then top with eight or nine banana slices and another crêpe. Continue layering with the filling and banana, ensuring the banana slices are in different positions each time, until you've used half the crêpes. Spread with ⅓ cup filling and another one-third of the pie crumb, then continue layering the crêpes with the filling and banana until you have one crêpe left. Spread with the remaining filling and pie crumb, then top with the final crêpe.

Cover with plastic wrap and refrigerate for 3 hours or overnight. Remove from the fridge 10 minutes before serving to soften slightly, then serve.

SERVES 10–12

400 ml (13½ fl oz) milk

4 eggs

60 g (2 oz) unsalted butter, melted, cooled, plus extra melted butter, to brush

150 g (5½ oz/1 cup) plain (all-purpose) flour

2 teaspoons caster (superfine) sugar

½ teaspoon fine salt

GRAHAM CRACKER PIE CRUMB

60 g (2 oz) graham crackers or digestive biscuits, finely ground

1 tablespoon golden caster (superfine) sugar (or organic cane sugar)

50 g (1¾ oz) unsalted butter, melted

BANANA CREAM FILLING

625 ml (21 fl oz/2½ cups) thickened (whipping) cream

175 g (6 oz/½ cup) sweetened condensed milk

50 g (1¾ oz/⅓ cup) pure icing (confectioners') sugar

1 teaspoon vanilla bean paste

3 bananas

Chocolate speculaas deliciousness

'How can anything be *this* delicious?' This is what I thought when I first tried Magnolia Bakery's famous banana cream pudding. What's more surprising is how easy it is to make, as is the whole category of American desserts called 'puddings', a variation of icebox cakes and so named for the custard (pudding) that's used to make them, along with whipped cream and cookies.

The three elements are layered and left to soften in the fridge, and the result is a decadent swirl of 'deliciousness'. The term, coined by LES bakeshop sugar Sweet sunshine for their must-try puds, so aptly describes this combo of dark chocolate custard and soft, spiced speculaas that I've used it for my own.

To make the chocolate custard, place the milk and sugar in a saucepan over medium heat and bring almost to the boil, stirring to dissolve the sugar. Meanwhile, place the cornflour in a bowl and gradually whisk in the cream, making sure there are no lumps, then whisk in the egg yolks. Whisking constantly, gradually add the milk mixture to the egg mixture. Return the mixture to the pan over medium heat and cook, whisking constantly, until it comes to the boil, then whisk for a further 2 minutes or until thickened. Remove from the heat. Add the chocolate and stand for 1 minute, then whisk until melted and combined. Whisk in the vanilla, then cover the surface with plastic wrap and refrigerate for 1 hour or until cold.

Preheat the oven to 180°C (350°F) and line two baking trays with baking paper.

To make the soft-baked speculaas, using an electric mixer, beat the butter and sugars for 3 minutes or until light and creamy. Sift the flour, bicarbonate of soda, baking powder, spices and salt into a bowl, then add to the butter mixture and beat on low speed until just combined. Roll into 3 cm (1¼ in) balls, then place, 5 cm (2 in) apart, on the prepared trays. Bake, swapping the trays halfway through, for 10–12 minutes or until cooked around the edges and soft in the centre. Cool slightly on the trays, then transfer to a wire rack to cool completely. Break into chunks.

To assemble, using an electric mixer, whisk the cream and icing sugar to stiff peaks. Place one-third of the speculaas over the base of a 3 litre (105 fl oz) bowl or trifle dish, then spread over half the chocolate custard and half the whipped cream. Repeat these layers, then top with the remaining speculaas. Cover with plastic wrap and refrigerate for at least 4 hours or up to 24 hours for the speculaas to soften and the flavours to infuse, then spoon into bowls to serve.

TIP *Speculaas (speculoos in Belgium), crisp, buttery Dutch cookies spiced with cinnamon, nutmeg, cloves and ginger, are available from gourmet food shops, and can be substituted here – just add extra softening time in the fridge as they're harder. You can also use the American version, biscoff – and, since we're talking, you have to try speculaas spread.*

SERVES 10–12

500 ml (17 fl oz/2 cups) thickened (whipping) cream
150 g (5½ oz/1 cup) pure icing (confectioners') sugar, sifted

CHOCOLATE CUSTARD
375 ml (12½ fl oz/1½ cups) milk
75 g (2¾ oz/⅓ cup) caster (superfine) sugar
1½ tablespoons cornflour (cornstarch)
125 ml (4 fl oz/½ cup) pouring (whipping/heavy) cream
2 egg yolks
125 g (4½ oz) dark chocolate (55% cocoa solids), finely chopped
1 teaspoon natural vanilla extract

SOFT-BAKED SPECULAAS
125 g (4½ oz) unsalted butter, chopped, softened
2 tablespoons caster (superfine) sugar
75 g (2¾ oz/⅓ cup firmly packed) light brown sugar
150 g (5½ oz/1 cup) plain (all-purpose) flour
½ teaspoon bicarbonate of soda (baking soda)
½ teaspoon baking powder
1½ teaspoons ground cinnamon
¾ teaspoon ground ginger
pinch each of ground allspice and freshly grated nutmeg
½ teaspoon fine salt

Apple & earl grey caramel crostatas

Apple pie, the sweet American icon, has a special place in Gotham's heart. With its cool clime and verdant pastures, New York State is the second-largest apple producer in the country. When apples are in season, farmers' markets heave with apple crates packed with more than twenty different varieties. It's a beautiful sight to behold.

Which brings us back to pie, the best home for abundant apples. In New York, you'll find it in every shape and form, from a classic double crust with cinnamon nutmeg at Bubby's to a cheekier version drizzled with candy-apple caramel at Butter & Scotch. At David Burke fabrick, the restaurant-take tarte tatin dubbed The Big Apple Tart is even embellished with a skyline-shaped cookie.

My own best apple pie moment was at hot new joint Upland, when a hidden earl grey caramel spilled out of a shortcrust apple crostata – *bliss*. These individual free-form pies follow in its footsteps, with a beguilingly floral caramel decadently drizzled on top.

To make the sweet shortcrust pastry, place the flour, icing sugar and baking powder in a food processor and process until combined. Add the butter and process until the mixture resembles breadcrumbs. Add the sour cream and process until the mixture just comes together in a large ball. Remove and shape into a disc, then wrap in plastic wrap and refrigerate for 1 hour.

Meanwhile, to make the oat crumble, combine the flour, sugar, salt and oats in a bowl. Using your fingers, rub the butter into the flour mixture until a dough forms. Set aside until needed.

Place the apple slices, sugar, flour and melted butter in a bowl and toss to combine.

Line a baking tray with baking paper. Divide the chilled pastry into six portions. Roll out one portion on a lightly floured work surface to a 3 mm (⅛ in) thick, 17 cm (6¾ in) round. Transfer to the prepared tray, then place one-sixth of the apple mixture in the centre of the pastry, leaving a 3 cm (1¼ in) border. Fold the pastry border over the apple mixture, roughly pleating the edges as you go, leaving the filling in the centre exposed. Scatter the oat crumble over the apple filling. Repeat with the remaining pastry, apple mixture and crumble, then freeze the pies for 30 minutes or until firm.

Preheat the oven to 180°C (350°F).

Bake the pies for 45 minutes or until the pastry and oat crumble are golden. Remove and cool for 10 minutes.

SERVES 6

3 pink lady apples, peeled, cored, finely sliced

75 g (2¾ oz/⅓ cup) caster (superfine) sugar

2 teaspoons plain (all-purpose) flour

20 g (¾ oz) unsalted butter, melted

double (extra-thick double/ clotted) cream or vanilla ice cream, to serve

SWEET SHORTCRUST PASTRY

260 g (9 oz/1¾ cups) plain (all-purpose) flour

50 g (1¾ oz/⅓ cup) pure icing (confectioners') sugar

⅓ teaspoon baking powder

200 g (7 oz) cold unsalted butter, roughly chopped

80 g (2¾ oz/⅓ cup) sour cream

OAT CRUMBLE

2 tablespoons plain (all-purpose) flour

2 tablespoons caster (superfine) sugar

pinch of fine salt

2 tablespoons rolled (porridge) oats

30 g (1 oz) unsalted butter, chopped, softened

EARL GREY CARAMEL

1 earl grey tea bag

60 ml (2 fl oz/¼ cup) boiling water

110 g (4 oz/½ cup) caster (superfine) sugar

125 ml (4½ oz/½ cup) pouring (whipping/heavy) cream

Meanwhile, to make the earl grey caramel, steep the tea bag in the boiling water for 4 minutes, then discard the tea bag. Pour the tea into a small saucepan and add the sugar. Bring to the boil over medium–high heat, stirring to dissolve the sugar, then cook, without stirring, for 7 minutes or until the caramel reaches 170°C (340°F) on a sugar thermometer (the dark tea makes it difficult to gauge by colour). Reduce the heat to low, then gradually add the cream (be careful as it will bubble up and spit) and whisk until smooth. Allow to cool completely.

Top the pies with thick cream or ice cream, then drizzle generously with the earl grey caramel and serve with the remaining caramel on the side.

TIP *You can also make this as one big free-form crostata (bake for an extra 10–15 minutes) and serve it whole with spoons for everyone to dig in.*

WASHINGTON
SQUARE PARK
18.26

Chocolate crack pie

I don't know who first coined the name, but Christina Tosi's legendary Crack Pie was my benchmark experience for something so addictive you just can't stop eating it. Then I tried Ample Hill's Salted Crack Caramel ice cream studded with sugar-crusted chocolate-covered saltines. *Seriously?*

Now that I'm an expert on the subject (aka addict) I can share that desserts that are a bomb of salty, caramel notes tend to qualify as crack, like this can't-stop-at-one-slice pie. It's a crumb-crust pie, another New York favourite made with everything from ground pretzels (Butter & Scotch) to oat cookies (Milk Bar) and used to house creamy fillings. Here, crunchy shards of caramelised crackers hold a rich just-set chocolate pudding, with salt flakes on top to set it all off.

Preheat the oven to 180°C (350°F) and grease a 23 cm (9 in) pie dish.

To make the crack crust, process 120 g (4½ oz) of the crackers in a food processor until finely ground. Using your hands, break the remaining 30 g (1 oz) of crackers into rough 1.5 cm (½ in) pieces, then add to the ground crackers. Place the butter and sugar in a saucepan over medium–high heat and cook, stirring occasionally, until the butter is melted and the mixture bubbles up. Remove from the heat and stir in the cracker crumbs until well combined. Working quickly before it hardens, press the crumb mixture into the base and sides of the pie dish (a flat-based cup helps smooth out any bumps), arranging most of the large pieces around sides and top. Bake for 15 minutes or until golden and crisp. Remove from the oven (if the crust has slumped, use the flat-based glass cup to press the mixture back into the base and sides; take care as the mixture is hot). Set aside to cool.

Reduce the oven temperature to 160°C (320°F).

Meanwhile, place the milk and dark chocolate in a heatproof bowl. Bring the cream and milk almost to the boil in a small saucepan, then pour over the chocolate. Stand for 3 minutes, then whisk until smooth. Allow to cool. Add the egg and whisk to combine, then strain the chocolate mixture through a fine sieve into the pie shell.

Bake for 30 minutes or until set around edges with a slight wobble in the centre. Set aside for 2 hours or until cooled completely, then scatter generously with salt flakes and serve.

SERVES 12

125 g (4½ oz) milk chocolate, finely chopped

125 g (4½ oz) dark chocolate (55% cocoa solids), finely chopped

125 ml (4½ fl oz/½ cup) pouring (whipping/heavy) cream

125 ml (4½ fl oz/½ cup) milk

1 egg, lightly beaten

sea salt flakes, to scatter

CRACK CRUST

150 g (5½ oz) Salada, saltines or soda crackers

180 g (6½ oz) unsalted butter, chopped

165 g (6 oz/¾ cup) golden caster (superfine) sugar (or organic cane sugar)

West Village

I prefer Dominique Ansel Kitchen in West Village to the original in Soho.
It's less busy and sells the best burrata soft serve in summer.

I never leave New York without one late-night session at Comedy Cellar.
I laugh so hard my face hurts.

The Stonewall Riots in 1969 prompted the national gay liberation movement.
You can see its legacy in WV's LGBT bars and counterculture.

Salted honey pie

Four & Twenty Blackbirds' signature pie. The richest, most perfect slice of heaven.

SWEET HONEY FILLING + ALL-BUTTER SHORTCRUST + A SMATTERING OF SEA SALT FLAKES +
LOADS OF WHIPPED CREAM

One day, honey was substituted for missing booze in a bourbon chess pie, and the rest is history.

The restaurant–diner

The original Bubby's in Tribeca opened over twenty-five years ago when the
neighbourhood was still a backwater. Now, it's all multi million–dollar lofts.
But Bubby's still feels like a neighbourhood place, which is the appeal (I'd wager for
the celebrities who dine here, too). There's also the sweet pie – it's famous for it –
made just like grandma would, and served à la mode.

Boozy blueberry, blackberry & rye pie

If there was a dessert that traced the passage of time, it would be sweet pie. Eaten year round, it's the one truly seasonal sweet, its fillings changing with the next crop of fruit and vegetables, the warmth or coolness of the weather, or an upcoming American holiday. Pie, you're cool like that.

In summer, it's all about pies bursting with luscious fruit: peaches, nectarines, sour cherries and the rainbow of berries. I'd never thought much of blueberries until I had them fresh, plump, firm and juicy in New York. It was a revelation really.

I ate them in pies too, with their crisp, flaky pastry and beautiful lattice tops. The best are found in Brooklyn – Four & Twenty Blackbirds, Butter & Scotch and The Blue Stove – where artisan pie shops channel the grandmas of America's south and keep them fruit forward. It's in this vein that I've made this nutty rye crust pie with a mix of blueberries and blackberries, and a generous splash of rye whisky to bring it all together.

To make the rye pastry, cut the butter and lard into 1 cm (½ in) pieces and freeze for 30 minutes to firm. Combine the water and vinegar in a small jug and refrigerate for 30 minutes.

Place the flours, sugar and salt in a food processor. Add the butter and lard, then process until pea-sized bits of fat remain. With the motor running, add the chilled water mixture and process until the pastry just comes together (there will be chunks of fat visible – this is a good thing!). Shape into two discs, one slightly larger than the other, and wrap in plastic wrap. Refrigerate for at least 1 hour.

Preheat the oven to 220°C (430°F) and grease a 23 cm (9 in) pie dish.

Roll out the larger dough disc on a lightly floured work surface until 3 mm (⅛ in) thick, then use to line the pie dish. Trim the pastry to 3 cm (1¼ in) beyond the rim of the dish, then refrigerate the pie shell until needed.

Roll out the remaining dough disc on a lightly floured surface until 3 mm (⅛ in) thick. Using a fluted pastry wheel, cut out 4 cm (1½ in) wide strips. Transfer to a baking tray lined with baking paper and refrigerate until needed.

Place the apple, blueberries, blackberries, lemon juice, whisky or bourbon, sugars, arrowroot and salt in a large bowl and toss to combine. Pour into the pie shell. Using the pastry strips, cover the top in a lattice pattern. Trim the pastry strips to align with the pastry base, then roll the pastry under itself to sit against the rim of the dish. Flute the edge with your fingers or crimp with a fork. Brush the pastry with eggwash, then scatter generously with the raw sugar.

SERVES 8

1 small granny smith apple, coarsely grated

350 g (12½ oz/2⅓ cups) blueberries

400 g (14 oz/2½ cups) blackberries

1 tablespoon lemon juice

2 tablespoons rye whisky or bourbon

110 g (4 oz/½ cup) caster (superfine) sugar

55 g (2 oz/¼ cup firmly packed) light brown sugar

2½ tablespoons arrowroot

½ teaspoon fine salt

1 egg, lightly beaten

raw (demerara) sugar, to scatter

whipped cream or vanilla ice cream, to serve

BUTTER + LARD RYE PASTRY

180 g (6½ oz) unsalted butter

70 g (2½ oz) lard

180 ml (6 fl oz/¾ cup) iced water

2 tablespoons cider vinegar

185 g (6½ oz/1¼ cups) plain (all-purpose) flour

185 g (6½ oz/1½ cups) rye flour

1 tablespoon caster (superfine) sugar

1 teaspoon fine salt

Place the pie dish on a baking tray and bake, rotating the dish halfway through, for 20 minutes. Reduce the oven temperature to 180°C (350°F) and bake for a further 30–40 minutes or until the pastry is golden and cooked through, and the juices are bubbling (cover the top with baking paper to prevent the edge overbrowning if necessary).

Remove the pie from the oven and cool on a wire rack for 2 hours to give the juices time to settle. Serve warm or at room temperature with whipped cream or vanilla ice cream.

TIPS *If you're using a metal pie dish, decrease the temperature by 15°C (60°F); if it's ceramic, increase it by the same amount. Fresh berries are best, but you can use frozen if they are out of season. Just thaw them first, and add an extra 2 tablespoons of arrowroot.*

BOOZY BLUEBERRY,
BLACKBERRY + RYE PIE

Pie crust with Emily & Melissa Elsen, Four & Twenty Blackbirds

HAND-MADE

Some people prefer a food processor, but we favour a hand-held pastry blender and flat-bottom bowl. Why deal with the storage and cleanup of a big machine that can over-blend ingredients? Plus, there's the gratification of making it with your own two hands.

USE HIGH-FAT BUTTER

The most important ingredient in a delicious pie crust is good, fresh butter. We use unsalted butter with a fat content of 82% or more, but standard unsalted butter will work. You can also use half butter, half good-quality rendered lard.

DON'T OVER-BLEND

Start cutting butter into the flour mixture with a bench scraper, then switch to a hand-held pastry blender.

Continue until it reaches a cornmeal-like consistency, leaving a few small butter chunks that get worked in by hand when you add water; don't overwork it.

RELAX

Don't forget dough needs to rest – and so do you. Once it's made, let the dough chill in the fridge so the moisture is absorbed by the flour. Meanwhile, prep the filling and enjoy a cup of tea, or even a glass of wine.

MAKE EXTRA

Don't hesitate to make a double or triple batch of crust and freeze it for later. Portion it into discs and wrap tightly in plastic wrap or place in freezer-proof bags. When you need it, thaw it at room temperature.

Kouign amann bread pudding

Kouign amann, the classic pastry from Brittany and pronounced *kween ahman*, is relatively obscure even in France. But in recent years it has shot to fame, courtesy of a few dedicated pastry chefs who resolved to make the delicieux but notoriously challenging pastry commercially available.

Dominique Ansel, whose 'DKA' (Dominique's Kouign Amann) was his best-selling item before the cronut, describes the calorific layers of caramelised sugar, salted butter and flaky pastry as a 'caramelised croissant', while others call it a 'croissant on steroids'. Around ten New York bakeries, from Épicerie Boulud to Bouchon Bakery, now turn them out.

Interestingly, you can replicate its flavours (i.e. cheat) in a bread pudding by using day-old croissants and a healthy dose of melted butter and sugar, the pudding's custard interior also mimicking a real kouign amann. This would be my number one choice of dessert to take to a dinner party in Manhattan. It's sophisticated yet comforting, and always a hit with New Yorkers, who just love bread pudding and kouign amann.

Preheat the oven to 180°C (350°F).

Melt 125 g (4½ oz) of the butter, then brush generously over the base and sides of a 25 cm (10 in) tart tin or pie dish. Reserve the remaining melted butter. Place 110 g (4 oz/½ cup) of the sugar in a small bowl, then scatter one-third of it over the base and sides of the tin or dish to coat, tipping the excess back into the bowl.

Using a sharp knife, cut the edges off the croissants in strips and use to line the base and sides of the tin or dish to form a pastry-like shell. Reserve the remaining edges and fluffy insides. Brush the croissant shell generously with some of the reserved melted butter, then scatter over another one-third of the sugar in the bowl.

Place the milk, cream and the remaining 100 g (3½ oz) of butter in a saucepan over medium heat and cook for 5 minutes or until the butter is melted and the mixture is warmed through. Whisk the eggs and the remaining 75 g (2¾ oz/⅓ cup) of sugar in a large bowl then, whisking constantly, gradually add the milk mixture and whisk until well combined.

Tear the fluffy insides of the croissants into rough chunks, then add to the custard and set aside for 3 minutes or until well soaked. Using a large spoon, carefully transfer the soaked mixture to the croissant shell. Pour over any remaining custard.

Top the pudding with the remaining croissant edges (it doesn't need to be flat – I use all the end bits), then brush over the rest of the reserved melted butter and scatter over the remaining sugar in the bowl.

Bake for 25 minutes or until the pudding is set and the sugar on top is crackly. Rest for 10 minutes, then serve with vanilla ice cream or whipped cream.

SERVES 8

225 g (8 oz) unsalted butter
185 g (6½ oz) caster (superfine) sugar
500 g (1 lb 2 oz) (about 6) croissants
250 ml (8½ fl oz/1 cup) milk
250 ml (8½ fl oz/1 cup) pouring (whipping/heavy) cream
4 eggs
vanilla ice cream or whipped cream, to serve

Hell's Kitchen

Also known as Clinton or Midtown West, but how can you beat Hell's Kitchen for a name? It was run by gangs (West Side Story) and Irish mobsters back in the day.

Sullivan Street Bakery is a little out of the way, but the bombolini are out of this world. I visit with hopes of chatting with owner/baker/philosopher Jim Lahey again.

On the Hudson River side of Hell's Kitchen is the Intrepid Sea, Air & Space Museum housed in a 1943 aircraft carrier. You'll love it if you're a nerd like me.

LOWER EAST SIDE
18.22

Hit list

Cupcake shops

Baked by Melissa

63 SPRING ST, NEW YORK (SOHO);
PLUS MORE LOCATIONS.

What's cuter than cupcakes? Little ones, and everybody goes crazy for them at Baked by Melissa. The bite-sized treats, just larger than a quarter and sold in citywide hole-in-the-walls, come in seasonally inspired flavours, such as lemon meringue pie and cotton candy. Don't miss the signature Tie Dye with rainbow sugar crystals.

Prohibition Bakery

9 CLINTON ST, NEW YORK (LES).

Classic cocktails inspire the range of mini cupcakes here, and top-shelf liquor infuses the cake base and frostings. Don't let the dainty size or pretty forms fool you – they pack a punch. I downed a handful, but kept coming back for more Pretzels & Beer.

sugar Sweet sunshine

126 RIVINGTON ST, NEW YORK (LES).

Cupcakes are the core business of this eccentric LES fixture. In combos like strawberry with whipped peanut butter mousse, they're more playful (and flavoursome) than your average cupcake, too. For me, the real star is the puddings, including Chocolate Chip Deliciousness, a crack-like mess of cookie bits, butterscotch pudding and whipped cream.

Sweet Revenge

62 CARMINE ST, NEW YORK (WEST VILLAGE).

If cutesy cupcakes don't float your boat, these guys might. More like flavour-packed muffins, the changing range features Crimson & Cream, an upmarket remake of red velvet drizzled with raspberry coulis. The cafe-restaurant-bar also pairs beer and wine with the sweet treats, which naturally makes them even better.

OTHER NOTABLES: Georgetown Cupcake, Molly's Cupcakes, Sprinkles Cupcakes.

Bakeries & patisseries

Amy's Bread

672 9TH AVE (HELL'S KITCHEN); CHELSEA MARKET, 75 9TH AVE (CHELSEA); 250 BLEECKER ST (WEST VILLAGE).

It's heartwarming Americana here with layer cakes that have been New York favourites since Amy's opened twenty-five years ago. The delicious red velvet, black and white, and yellow cake with pink frosting are the soft-crumbed towering signatures and also available in cute cupcake form.

Baked

359 VAN BRUNT ST, BROOKLYN (RED HOOK); 279 CHURCH ST, NEW YORK (TRIBECA).

Cupcakes and layer cakes are also bestsellers at this cult Brooklyn bakery (see *Bars*, page 59) and they're as pretty as can be. I haven't tried them all – there are over thirty rotating flavours, from funfetti to Red Hook velvet – but I can vouch for the inventive Malted Milk Ball infused with ale, and the Sweet & Salty, with salted caramel and chocolate.

Bakeri

150 WYTHE AVE, BROOKLYN (WILLIAMSBURG); 105 FREEMAN ST, BROOKLYN (GREENPOINT).

I can't tell you how many recommendations I received from those-in-the-know for this quaint neighbourhood bakery-cafe. Rustic baked goods, from challah, glazed lemon cake and gâteau Basque to the best little brownies, are served on vintage plates, and waitresses wear retro mechanic uniforms. It's charm and flavour in spades.

Billy's Bakery

184 9TH AVE, NEW YORK (CHELSEA); 75 FRANKLIN ST, NEW YORK (TRIBECA); PLUS TWO MORE LOCATIONS.

Classic American cupcakes, layer cakes and icebox pies are celebrated at Billy's, as is yesteryear, with sweet retro decor adding to the 'just like your grandma made it' flavour of the baked goods. For perfect crumb and buttercream frosting, aka simple done well, head here.

Burrow

68 JAY ST, BROOKLYN (DUMBO).

At this gem of a patisserie, you'll find delicate cakes with French and Japanese influences, from regional specialities of Breton and gâteau Basque to Japanese strawberry shortcake and cotton-soft cheesecake. (Also, see *Cookies*, page 59 and *Pastries*, page 102).

Eileen's Special Cheesecake

17 CLEVELAND PL, NEW YORK (NOLITA).

Whenever this is mentioned, my brother's ears prick up; it's his all-time go-to cheesecake. The light, fluffy rendition has been around for forty years and is consistently on must-try lists. My bro adores the blueberry fruit-topped takes, while I go classic, but there are around thirty different flavours and sizes from tart (mini) to large.

Lady M Cake Boutique

41 E 78TH ST, NEW YORK (UES); 36 W 40TH ST, NEW YORK (MIDTOWN); PLUS THREE MORE LOCATIONS.

J'adore this French-persuasion patisserie, from the chic minimalist design to the elegant remakes of classic desserts, from vanilla-chocolate Checkers to Banana Mille Feuille. The Mille Crêpes – twenty wafer-thin layers with superb pastry cream – comes in eight flavours including the striking green tea, but my pick is the original. Dine in; it's an experience.

Magnolia Bakery

401 BLEECKER ST, NEW YORK (WEST VILLAGE); PLUS FIVE MORE LOCATIONS.

It's the bakeshop that ignited a worldwide cupcake phenomenon and even cameoed in *Sex and The City*. Hordes (beware!) still queue for the pretty little sweets and delicious retro-styled American desserts, such as red velvet, chocolate icebox and caramel-pecan cheesecake, but the categorical standout is banana pudding. I'd line up in the snow for an hour (and did) for a single sumptuous bite.

Mah-Ze-Dahr

28 GREENWICH AVE, NEW YORK (WEST VILLAGE).

Tom Colicchio and Oprah are among the big-name fans of baker Umber Ahmad, who up until recently was only selling her rustic sweets wholesale and online. Now, you can find the whole range, from salted caramel cashew tart to lemon meringue cake, at her sparkly new bricks and mortar shop. It opened just after I left. Intel on the ground gives it a big thumbs up.

Momofuku Milk Bar

251 E 13TH ST, NEW YORK (EAST VILLAGE), PLUS SIX MORE LOCATIONS.

Crack pie: the name says it all. The oat cookie crust, gooey butter-filled concoction is also the only pie on the menu at dessert kingpin Christina Tosi's sweet den – further proof of its awesomeness. There are plenty of other habit-forming desserts (see *Cookies*, page 60, and *Ice Cream*, page 186), and you can get a fix at most locations until midnight.

Ovenly

31 GREENPOINT AVE, BROOKLYN (GREENPOINT).

This much-loved cafe–bakery in Brooklyn turns out rustic sweets (see *Cookies*, page 60) and layer cakes with a twist. The celebrated Brooklyn blackout uses black cocoa and Brooklyn Brewery stout to achieve its signature midnight hue and grown-up flavour, making it my choice in an all-star line up that also includes carrot cake with honey buttercream.

Rice To Riches

37 SPRING ST, NEW YORK (NOLITA).

A whole space-age emporium dedicated to rice pudding was revolutionary fourteen years ago, but the idea quickly caught on, turning the comfort food from an at-home treat to a New York sweet staple. It's not the preserve of purely traditional flavours either, with cheeky and delicious combinations like Sex Drugs and Rocky Road (my pick), and 'Oreo' gasm.

Two Little Red Hens

1652 2ND AVE, NEW YORK (UES).

It looks just like grandma's house – and tastes like it, too. The New York cheesecake is on just about every top ten list, while the Brooklyn Blackout sets the benchmark for chocolate pudding fudge cake indulgence. It's available as a cupcake, or go the small cake – try as you might, you won't stop at one slice. The apple, pecan and banana cream pies are also sensational.

Veniero's

342 E 11TH ST, NEW YORK (EAST VILLAGE).

The cheesecake at Veniero's is light as air yet rich and creamy, and outstanding. It's also among the top five in New York; no mean feat in the city that immortalised it. The iconic Italian pasticceria also turns out homeland classics, including cannoli, and the old-school decor has to be seen to be believed.

Pie shops

Four & Twenty Blackbirds

439 3RD AVE, BROOKLYN (GOWANUS); BROOKLYN PUBLIC LIBRARY, 10 GRAND ARMY PLAZA, BROOKLYN.

Believe the hype: these could be NYC's pre-eminent pies. A signature all-butter crust and seasonal produce are at the heart of what makes them so good, plus a mix of tradition and innovation. Think green chilli chocolate, buttermilk chess, salted caramel apple and my all-time fave, salted honey. Topped with thick whipped cream, you'll never look at pie the same way again.

Petee's Pie Company

61 DELANCEY ST, NEW YORK (LES).

Grab a piece of the Brooklyn pie action on the Lower East Side at this cute little pie shop, where ingredients are locally sourced, pie flavours are produce-driven and a flaky crust is all important. The year-round hit is the salty chocolate chess pie.

Steve's Authentic Key Lime Pies

185 VAN DYKE ST, BROOKLYN (RED HOOK).

Pretty much unanimously agreed as the best key lime pies in the city, Steve Tarpin has been making his the same way for over twenty years – with freshly squeezed juice, chilled and unembellished. The quirky commissary shop sells them in all manner of sizes, along with chocolate-dipped versions on sticks known as Swingles.

The Blue Stove

415 GRAHAM AVE, BROOKLYN (WILLIAMSBURG).

My mum and I became a little obsessed with this charming, small-batch pie shop with some of the best pastry in town. Best sellers are the rich chocolate pecan and silky chocolate mousse pies, but I can't go past the seasonal fruit numbers, particularly the peach pie, which is just sensational.

Diners

Bubby's

120 HUDSON ST, NEW YORK (TRIBECA);
73 GANSEVOORT ST, NEW YORK (CHELSEA).

This good-lookin' diner and local celeb hangout began life as a pie company, which explains why the daily range is so good. That and the generous use of butter in their shortcrusts, and local-produce fillings. Apple, sour cherry and banoffee are among the classics, and at the High Line location, you can (must!) pair it with Ample Hills ice cream.

Butter & Scotch

818 FRANKLIN AVE, BROOKLYN (CROWN HEIGHTS).

There's everything to love here. One, it's a bakery *and* bar. That means cocktails come with slabs of the best pie or wedges of birthday cake so good I had to get the recipe (see page 120). It also means booze in said pies (such as bourbon ginger pecan) and shakes (see *Drinks*, page 186). The fitout is 1950s rockabilly, as is the cool vibe, so block off a brunch or evening and tuck in.

The Dutch

131 SULLIVAN ST, NEW YORK (SOHO).

Consistently on Gotham's Best Pies lists, this Soho clubhouse dishes up generous wedges with perfectly bronzed crusts and seasonal fruit fillings. Pecan pie, the delicious mainstay, gets the extra-special treatment, served with banana ice cream and a dousing of chocolate sauce.

Restaurants

L'Artusi

228 W 10TH ST, NEW YORK (WEST VILLAGE).

I can't recall who recommended this intimate Italian restaurant and its signature olive oil cake drizzled with golden raisin marmelata and paired with crème fraîche mousse, but whoever you are, thank you! It was equal parts rustic and sophisticated, and by the looks of the menu, all its dolci are, too.

Peter Luger Steak House

178 BROADWAY, BROOKLYN (WILLIAMSBURG).

Most people head to this NYC institution for the lauded steak, but those in the know come for cheesecake – the city's superlative offering, and the best thus far of my life. It's the rich, creamy mouthfeel, the nutty, caramel quality to the base, and the decadent dose (almost the size of the slice) of German schlag – thick whipped cream – that it comes with. The pecan pie is also outstanding.

The Polo Bar

1 E 55TH ST, NEW YORK (MIDTOWN EAST).

You'll be hard-pressed to get a seat (book way in advance) and there are far more spectacular NYC desserts, but the dining experience here is something special. It's fashion designer Ralph Lauren's restaurant-showroom and, as you'd expect, it looks like something out of a magazine. Likewise, service is old-world, elegant, even theatrical. Go for the walnut brownie à la mode, finished tableside with warm chocolate sauce.

Untitled (at the Whitney Museum)

99 GANSEVOORT ST, NEW YORK (CHELSEA).

At the glam eatery, nostalgia informs acclaimed pastry chef Miro Uskokovic's desserts (he's also behind the sweets at Gramercy Tavern). Think old-school milk and cookies (see *Cookies*, page 61), as well as a daily towering layer cake, served by the slice in grown-up combinations such as banana and concord grape, green tea and almond, and caramelised custard and honeycomb brittle.

Upland

345 PARK AVE S, NEW YORK (NOMAD).

This hip restaurant espousing west-coast produce and easy breezy Californian cuisine makes rustic desserts worth dining for. Milk + Cookies takes up permanent residence on the menu, but my pick is the signature crostata, which subs in new fruit each season – in winter, honey crisp apples with earl grey caramel; summer, strawberry and rhubarb with basil ice cream.

Vinegar Hill House

72 HUDSON AVE, BROOKLYN (VINEGAR HILL).

Nicole, a food-loving New Yorker, introduced to me to this charming, produce-driven restaurant, whose dessert ended up among my faves. It could be that I like simple done well and flavour drawn from each ingredient, which is just what their delectable buttermilk custard with peaches and basil, and chocolate Guinness cake have to offer.

Ice cream & drinks

Hot summer days

DAY 63, DESSERT 259: BRIOCHE ICE-CREAM
SANDWICH, ODDFELLOWS ICE CREAM CO,
WILLIAMSBURG

It was mid August and New York was still sweltering.
Hot town, summer in the city … The song's famous lyrics
were playing over and over in my head. *Walking on the
sidewalk, hotter than a match head …* Okay, I get why
everyone skips town and heads to the Hamptons now.
It also goes a long way to explain why ice cream, soft
serves, sundaes, shakes and floats are such a big thing.

Like a host of other New York desserts, creamy cooling
things have undergone a renaissance in recent years,
as new producers have geeked out, so to speak, on the
process. The use of local dairy products (New York State
has some of the best – think verdant pastures for cows
to graze on) was the first and most important change.
Ronnybrook Farm and Battenkill Valley are favourites
and you'll see their names highlighted around town.

Exploring the frontiers of new flavours and forms has
been another change, from exotic ingredients such as olive
oil, durian and lemon charcoal, to binge food mix-ins –
pretzels, potato chips, cereal, rice krispies and cola –
and even smash-ups: pies blended into shakes, waffle
cones forged from churros, and croissants sandwiching
ice cream.

All-artisan is all-important too, even with the traditionally
commercial stuff, and if it's not made inhouse, it's sourced
from another speciality producer. Collabs of this sort,
and on a larger scale – players teaming up to create a new
flavour – take place all the time in New York, and it kinda
makes the heart swell to see a big city fostering a sense
of community.

When my husband and daughter finished a five-scoop
waffle-boat banana split in 10 minutes flat, it occurred to
me that we were averaging at least one a day and another
at night (I swear those ice-cream carts and soft serve
trucks were following us!). I have never eaten so much
ice cream in my life.

« Like a host of other New York desserts, creamy cooling things have undergone a renaissance in recent years as new producers have 'geeked out' on the process. »

Ample Hills Creamery's The Munchies

Of them all – and this is tough, because New York's selection of ice cream is second to none – The Munchies at Ample Hills Creamery could be my favourite. Imagine all your guilty pleasures (salted pretzels, Ritz crackers, potato chips and M&Ms) set against a backdrop of more pretzel-infused ice cream for the ultimate creamy, crunchy, sweet, salty indulgence.

It's Brian Smith's top pick, too. He's the ice-cream mastermind behind Ample Hills, along with his wife Jackie Cuscuna, and they kindly shared the recipe from *Ample Hills Creamery: Secrets and Stories from Brooklyn's Favorite Ice Cream Shop* (Stewart, Tabori & Chang). I can't recommend this smart, fun cookbook enough, and the inventive flavours within its pages (Ooey Gooey Butter Cake runs a close second). At their beloved ice creamery, with locations all around the city, you can even opt for a pretzel or chocolate chip cone, but I like my ice cream in a classic waffle, which lets it shine.

Place the milk in a large saucepan over medium–high heat and warm, stirring occasionally, for 10–15 minutes or until it starts to steam. Remove the pan from the heat and stir in the pretzels. Cover the pan and steep the pretzels for 20 minutes. Pour the mixture through a fine sieve into a bowl, pressing down on the pretzels to extract as much milk as possible (don't worry if some of the pretzel 'pulp' pushes through into ice cream; that's totally okay). Return the pretzel-infused milk to the saucepan.

Prepare an ice bath in the sink or in a large heatproof bowl. Add the sugar and skim milk powder to the pretzel-infused milk and whisk until smooth, making sure the skim milk powder is wholly dissolved into the mixture and no lumps remain (any remaining sugar granules will dissolve over the heat). Stir in the cream. Clip a sugar thermometer to the saucepan and set the pan over medium heat. Cook, stirring often with a rubber spatula and scraping the bottom of the pan to prevent sticking and burning, for 5–10 minutes or until the mixture reaches 45°C (110°F). Remove the pan from the heat.

Place the egg yolks in a bowl. Whisking constantly, gradually pour 125 ml (4 fl oz/ ½ cup) of the hot milk mixture into the egg yolks to temper them. Continue to whisk slowly until the mixture is an even colour and consistency, then whisk the egg yolk mixture back into the remaining milk mixture. Return the pan to medium heat and cook, stirring often, for a further 5–10 minutes or until it reaches 75°C (165°F).

Transfer the pan to the prepared ice bath and cool, stirring occasionally, for 15–20 minutes. Pour the ice-cream base through a fine sieve into a storage container and refrigerate for 1–2 hours or until completely cool.

MAKES 1 LITRE

720 ml (24½ fl oz) milk

90 g (3 oz/1½ cups) mini salted pretzels

150 g (⅔ cup) organic cane sugar (or golden caster sugar)

60 g (2 oz) skim milk powder

400 ml (13½ fl oz) pouring (whipping/heavy) cream

2 egg yolks

MUNCHIES MIX-IN

40 g (1½ oz/1 generous cup) Ritz crackers

60 g (2 oz/1 generous cup) salted mini pretzels

30 g (1 oz/1 generous cup) salted potato chips

60 g (2 oz) skim milk powder

200 g (7 oz) organic cane sugar (or golden caster sugar)

120 g (4½ oz) unsalted butter, melted

225 g (8 oz/1 generous cup) M&Ms, chopped

Meanwhile, preheat the oven to 135°C (275°F) and line a baking tray with baking paper.

To make the munchies mix-in, place the crackers, pretzels and potato chips in a large bowl and, using your hands, break into pieces about a quarter of their original size – the goal here isn't to pulverise them into dust (though a little dust is okay, as it will help bind everything together later on). Add the skim milk powder and sugar, and toss to combine. Pour over the butter and work the mixture together with your hands, squeezing it into clumps and breaking it apart, almost like kneading dough. Spread the mixture out evenly on the prepared tray and bake for 20 minutes or until the mixture just begins to toast and turn brown. Set aside to cool completely.

Transfer the cooled base to an ice-cream maker and churn according to the manufacturer's instructions. Transfer the ice cream to a storage container, folding in the munchies mix-in and M&Ms as you go. Use as much of the mix-in as you want; you won't necessarily need the whole batch. Serve immediately or harden in the freezer for 8–12 hours for a more scoopable ice cream.

TIP *When I made this I only used about half the mix-in. Naturally, I used it as an excuse to make another delicious batch of ice cream.*

Greenpoint

*It's Brooklyn's northernmost neighbourhood and a Polish enclave.
It's gentrifying, but still has a yesteryear feel to it.*

*When I went to Ovenly for rosemary and currant scones, I could see
East Village just across the river (above). It seemed so close.*

*I've not yet been to Lomzynianka, but I hear the food is really good,
particularly the kielbasa sausage.*

Dumbo

An acronym for Down Under Manhattan Bridge Overpass. It was deserted until tech companies and luxe real estate set up camp. Now, it's real hip.

Burrow is small, but so charming. I'd always order a Kettl sencha and a roasted green tea cookie, and sit on the one seat in the shop.

For Manhattan Bridge photo ops, the best spot is Washington and Water Streets (above), while Brooklyn Flea is the place for Brooklyn Bridge.

Olive oil & mandarin gelato

Before I set off for New York, I trawled through every Best Dessert list I could find in every magazine and blog. Consistently, OTTO's olive oil gelato was mentioned. The unique flavour has been on the menu at Mario Batali's beloved Washington Square Italian restaurant since it opened nearly fifteen years ago, varying only with seasonal accompaniments. On our visit, it was paired with passionfruit granita, pomegranate sauce and pine nut brittle. We came back not long after for another one.

The revelatory flavour has also inspired a legion of sweet purveyors, including Marta's olive oil affogato with honeycomb and cumquat, Narcissa's winter sundae with olive oil ice cream and Meyer lemon curd, and Big Gay Ice Cream's olive oil soft serve.

My rendition is adapted from the restaurant's original recipe, but with more olive oil to play off the mandarin syrup I've swirled in. Make sure to use the best EVOO you can. For a plated dessert, segments of fresh mandarin and candied hazelnuts would go nicely.

Prepare an ice bath in the sink or in a large heatproof bowl.

Place the milk, sugar and salt in a saucepan over medium heat and bring almost to the boil, stirring to dissolve the sugar. Place the egg yolks in a heatproof bowl and whisk to combine. Whisking constantly, gradually add the milk mixture.

Return the mixture to the pan and stir constantly over medium heat for 6 minutes or until the mixture reaches 75°C (165°F) or is thick enough to coat the back of a spoon.

Transfer the pan to the ice bath and cool, stirring occasionally, for 20 minutes, then whisk in the cream and olive oil. Strain through a fine sieve into a container, then cover and refrigerate for 2 hours or until cold.

Meanwhile, to make the mandarin syrup, place the sugar, mandarin juice and water in a saucepan over medium–high heat. Bring to the boil, stirring until the sugar dissolves, then cook for 8 minutes or until reduced and syrupy.

Churn the base in an ice-cream maker according to the manufacturer's instructions. Transfer half the ice cream to an airtight container, then pour over half the mandarin syrup and swirl once to combine. Repeat this process with the remaining ice cream and syrup, then freeze for 4 hours or until firm. Drizzle with extra olive oil and scatter with sea salt flakes to serve.

MAKES 600 ML (20½ FL OZ)

375 ml (12½ fl oz/1½ cups) milk
110 g (4 oz/½ cup) caster (superfine) sugar
¼ teaspoon fine salt
5 egg yolks
125 ml (4 fl oz/½ cup) pouring (whipping/heavy) cream
2 tablespoons extra virgin olive oil, plus extra to drizzle
sea salt flakes, to scatter

MANDARIN SYRUP
110 g (4 oz/½ cup) caster (superfine) sugar
125 ml (4 fl oz/½ cup) mandarin juice (from about 3 mandarins)
60 ml (2 fl oz/¼ cup) water

Jessica, social media manager

'I think of my favourite sweet as the one thing I could never get sick of and that is Big Gay Ice Cream's Monday Sundae. A lot of New York desserts take it one step too far, but this is just at the right point. It's the perfect dessert.'

The food truck/shop

Big Gay Ice Cream's bricks and mortar shop in East Village was on my way home, so I'd go there often for one of my favourite flavours: Salty Pimp or Apple Gobbler. I don't know what it is about ice cream generally, but the staff always seem to be punk rockers or rockabilly kids. It's the same here.

Cucumber & mint popsicles

Popsicles, ice pops, ice blocks or ice lollies – whatever you call them, they're up there as a favourite in New York's sweet frozen arsenal to beat the summer heat. Carts and stands take up seasonal residence in every big park, food fair and flea market, so they're always on hand when you want something light and refreshing. The city is great like that.

People's Pops, which also turns out shaved-to-order ice drenched in housemade fruit syrup, is one of the biggest players, along with La Newyorkina, which is the best in my book and specialises in the wonderful Mexican street food variety known as paletas. My best friend Mel, a popsicle-lover who visited over summer, couldn't resist each time we saw one and together we sampled a rainbow of inventive flavours: mango-chilli, fresh coconut, sour cherry, rhubarb-jasmine and more.

These delectable cucumber, mint and lemon popsicles follow New York's lead with seasonal produce and little else, and taste blissfully pure and fresh.

Place the sugar and water in a small saucepan and bring to the boil over medium–high heat, stirring to dissolve the sugar. Remove from the heat and cool completely. Stir in the lemon juice.

Place the cucumber and sugar syrup in a food processor and process to a fine purée, then pass through a fine sieve, pressing to extract the liquid. Discard the solids.

Divide the mint leaves among six 100 ml (3½ fl oz) popsicle moulds, then pour over the cucumber liquid (there may be a little left over) and insert a stick in each. Freeze for 3 hours or until frozen, then serve.

TIP *For grown-ups, freeze the mixture into large ice cubes and serve with gin on the rocks.*

MAKES 6

165 g (6 oz/¾ cup) caster (superfine) sugar

375 ml (12½ fl oz/1½ cups) water

2½ tablespoons lemon juice

1½ (about 500 g/1 lb 2 oz) telegraph cucumbers, ends trimmed, sliced

2–3 mint sprigs (preferably with small leaves), leaves picked

RED HOOK
17.32

French toast ice-cream sandwiches

I don't know if the ice-cream sandwich has always been a thing in New York, but it was one of the biggest hits the summer we were in town. I'd never seen so many before, and in such wild forms. From macaron shells (François Payard) and brownies (Morgenstern's) to croissants (Union Fare), babka (Russ & Daughters) and doughnuts (Underwest and Ice & Vice) it was as if people were throwing ice cream into just about everything sweet, and often drizzling fudge sauce on top. Even the classic can be customised with different cookies and crazy crumbs to coat the edges (OddFellows). It was *so* much fun.

My OTT ice-cream sandwich takes a soft brioche bun, coats it in cornflakes, then finishes it off as custardy French toast. Filled with your pick of ice cream, it's warm-cold-soft-crunchy heaven.

Place the eggs, milk, cream and vanilla in a shallow bowl and whisk until well combined. Place the cornflakes in a separate shallow bowl and set both bowls aside.

Fill a frying pan 1 cm (½ in) deep with canola oil and heat over medium heat. Place one brioche in the egg mixture and soak well for 1 minute, then turn over and soak for a further 1 minute. Place the brioche in the cornflakes and turn to coat well. Carefully transfer to the oil and fry for 45–60 seconds or until golden. Carefully turn over and fry for a further 45–60 seconds or until golden and crisp. Drain on a plate lined with paper towel and cool slightly. Meanwhile, repeat with the remaining brioche until they are all crisp and golden.

Make an incision in the top of each bun to form a pocket. Fill with two scoops of ice cream, then scatter over the chopped peanuts. Drizzle with honey, if desired, and serve immediately.

MAKES 4

2 eggs

125 ml (4 fl oz/½ cup) milk

2 tablespoons pouring (whipping/heavy) cream

1 teaspoon natural vanilla extract

80 g (2¾ oz/2 cups) cornflakes, roughly crushed, leaving some whole flakes

canola oil, to shallow-fry

4 brioche buns

8 scoops of vanilla or your favourite ice cream

roughly chopped toasted peanuts, to scatter

honey, to drizzle (optional)

Ice cream with Brian Smith, Ample Hills Creamery

POWDER POWER

Milk and cream at the base level is water – 95% and 60% respectively. You need water's freezing properties to make ice cream, but the more water there is, the icier the ice cream will be. Skim milk powder adds all of the milk solids without the milk water and absorbs some of the water in milk, too.

GET CRANKING

Embrace an old-fashioned hand-cranked ice and rock salt ice-cream maker. It's a lot more fun and the hard work breeds community. Technically, it also makes better ice cream. The rock salt and ice slurry is far colder than the compressor in a home ice-cream maker, and drops the temperature more quickly, producing smaller ice crystals and a creamier finish.

ICE COLD

Store ice cream in the coldest spot in the freezer. Our commercial freezer keeps ice cream at −29°C (−20°F), but most home freezers range from −18°C to −15°C (0−5°F), and that state allows ice crystals to grow.

EGGCELLENT

If you don't have an allergy, using egg yolks as an emulsifier is an easy way to add texture to ice cream. The trick is using just enough to serve as an emulsifier without making it taste eggy. Usually 1.5–2% by volume of the recipe is the magic spot.

BoCoCa

An acronym for Boerum Hill, Cobble Hill and Carroll Gardens in Brooklyn.
It's three neighbourhoods really, all leafy, literary and really lovely.

I loved watching the afternoon swarm of children at Brooklyn Farmacy & Soda
Fountain. Their excitement for sundaes and floats was contagious.

Bergen Street is great for window shopping and people watching. There's everything
from boutique labels to homeware shops, and cool kids hanging around.

Campfire shakes (aka burnt marshmallow & Nutella)

New York makes a mean shake. Firstly, it uses quality ingredients – creamy local milk from Battenkill and Ronnybrook, and artisan ice cream by the likes of Big Gay and OddFellows. Secondly, you ain't seen flavours like this, from Morgenstern's black licorice to Davey's speculaas choc chip. At Butter & Scotch, they even blend a piece of pie or cake into your shake, or add a generous slug of liquor. Finally, the reckless abandon, loaded with ice cream, piled high with whipped cream and, in the case of Instagram sensation Black Tap, dripping with doughnuts, fudge and malt balls. This is America, after all.

This shake is made from ice cream with the sweet and smoky flavours of scorched marshmallow. It rocks as a stand-alone ice cream, but blend it with just a dash of milk, so it's basically thick ice-cream slurry, then top it with thick cream, more toasted marshmallows and a coating of Nutella, and you get an outrageous shake with the nostalgic flavours of campfire treats from your youth.

Preheat the oven to 180°C (350°F) and line the base and sides of a rimmed baking tray with baking paper.

To make the ice cream, spread the marshmallows over the prepared tray and bake for 15 minutes or until dark brown, with some marshmallows almost burnt (they will puff up and form a big mass, then deflate). Set aside to cool and harden, then break into small pieces.

Place the milk, sugar and salt in a saucepan over medium heat and bring almost to the boil, stirring to dissolve the sugar. Place the egg yolks in a heatproof bowl and whisk to combine then, whisking constantly, gradually add the milk mixture. Return the mixture to the pan and cook over low heat, stirring constantly, for 5 minutes or until the mixture reaches 75°C (165°F) or is thick enough to coat the back of a spoon. Remove from the heat, then add the burnt marshmallow pieces and whisk until the marshmallows are melted and combined (this may take up to 10 minutes). Strain the mixture through a fine sieve, then whisk in the cream. Cover and refrigerate for 1–2 hours or until cold. Churn in an ice-cream maker according to the manufacturer's instructions, then transfer to an airtight container and freeze for 3 hours or until firm.

Generously coat about 2.5 cm (1 in) down the inside of two 360 ml (12 fl oz) milkshake glasses with Nutella and set aside. Remove the ice cream from the freezer and set aside until just melted at the edges. Transfer to a blender, add the milk and pulse two or three times to break up the ice cream. Using a spatula, mash the mixture onto the blades, then continue pulsing, stopping and mashing, until the mixture is just blended and thick – you don't want it runny.

Divide evenly between the prepared glasses and top with whipped cream. If you are using the marshmallows, scorch them with a kitchen blowtorch until they are almost burnt (alternatively, scorch them under a hot grill). Cool slightly, then use to garnish the thickshake. Serve immediately.

MAKES 2 MILKSHAKES ... THAT'LL FEED 4

Nutella, to coat
250 ml (8½ fl oz/1 cup) milk
250 ml (8½ fl oz/1 cup) thickened (whipping) cream, whipped
6–8 white marshmallows (optional)

BURNT MARSHMALLOW ICE CREAM

150 g (5½ oz) white marshmallows
500 ml (17 fl oz/2 cups) milk
110 g (4 oz/½ cup) caster (superfine) sugar
¼ teaspoon fine salt
5 egg yolks
250 ml (8½ fl oz/1 cup) pouring (whipping/heavy) cream

BUTTER & SCOTCH,
CROWN HEIGHTS
11.39

Williamsburg

It's Brooklyn's most famous neighbourhood, and a lot of fun. It's more commercial than it used to be, but the hipster vibe lives on.

Smorgasburg is a heap of fun but it can get really hot and crowded. Tip: get there just as it opens, when the sun is milder and New Yorkers are still contemplating getting up.

I fell in love with Devoción. There's a waterfall of green plants at the back and they drown scoops of Davey's ice cream in their amazing coffee.

Red Hook

Red Hook was one of the country's busiest shipping centres and the big warehouses are now home to distilleries, commissaries and other artisan producers. It's industrial-meets-cool.

At Steve's Authentic Key Lime Pies, the pies are best chilled, so I would eat mine out front and watch them restore motorbikes next door.

One Sunday, we caught the 'Ikea' ferry to Red Hook, had lunch at Hometown BBQ, and admired the Statue of Liberty. It's the best view in the city.

El Caballero sundae

The only thing better than a New York ice cream is a sundae. As you'd imagine, they're *epic*. Think Davey's five-scoop, four-toppings banana split in a waffle cone boat, Morgenstern's Japanese raw milk ice-cream toast dripping with honey, Big Gay's soft serve Apple Gobbler, Quality Eats' Birthday Cake complete with a candle, and much, *much* more.

Likewise, this sundae starts with elegant individual components – salted caramel ice cream, dulce de leche, whipped cream, hot churros and orange-flecked chocolate – that are layered, swirled, drizzled and stacked into a sundae-slash-bonanza. I've dubbed it El Caballero, the Spanish cowboy, because no New York sundae is complete without a cool name. If you don't have time to make your own you can substitute store-bought dulce de leche, churros or cinnamon doughnuts, and caramel or vanilla ice cream, and it's just as good.

Prepare an ice bath in the sink or in a large heatproof bowl.

To make the ice cream, place the sugar in a saucepan over medium–high heat and cook, stirring often, until the sugar is completely melted. Cook, without stirring, until it turns a light-to-medium caramel colour (this will happen quickly, so watch closely; you don't want a dark caramel flavour for this ice cream). Immediately reduce the heat to medium and stir in the butter (be careful as it will bubble up and spit), then continue stirring until the mixture is smooth and combined. Stirring constantly, gradually pour in the cream (be careful as it will bubble up and spit again), then stir until combined. Stir in the salt and milk.

Whisk the egg yolks in a heatproof bowl until well combined. Whisking constantly, gradually add 125 ml (4 fl oz/½ cup) of the milk mixture and whisk until well combined. Add the egg mixture to the milk mixture in the pan and cook, stirring, for 5 minutes or until the mixture reaches 75°C (165°F) or is thick enough to coat the back of a spoon.

Transfer the pan to the ice bath and cool, stirring occasionally, for 20 minutes, then strain through a fine sieve into a container and refrigerate for 2 hours or until cold. Churn in an ice-cream maker according to the manufacturer's instructions, then transfer to a container and freeze for 3 hours or until frozen. Makes 1 litre.

recipe continued »

MAKES 4–6

395 g (14 oz) dulce de leche
(see tip, page 174)

600 ml (10½ fl oz) thickened
(whipping) cream, whipped to
stiff peaks with 2 tablespoons
icing (confectioners') sugar

100 g (3½ oz) fine dark chocolate
bar, such as Lindt Orange
Intense, broken into squares

SALTED CARAMEL ICE CREAM

330 g (11½ oz/1½ cups) caster
(superfine) sugar

60 g (2 oz) unsalted butter,
chopped

250 ml (9 fl oz/1 cup) pouring
(whipping/heavy) cream

½ teaspoon fine salt

500 ml (17 fl oz/2 cups) milk

6 egg yolks

To make the churros, fill a deep fryer or saucepan one-third full of canola oil and heat over medium heat to 180°C (350°F). Place the butter, sugar, salt and water in a small saucepan over medium heat and bring to the boil, stirring to melt the butter. Add the flour and cook, stirring constantly, for 2–3 minutes or until the mixture comes together in a ball. Transfer to the bowl of an electric mixer and beat for 2 minutes or until cool to the touch, then add the egg and beat until well combined. Transfer to a piping (icing) bag fitted with a 1.5 cm (½ in) star nozzle.

In batches of four or five, pipe 10 cm (4 in) lengths of dough into the oil and cook, turning occasionally, for 3 minutes or until golden. Remove with a slotted spoon and drain on paper towel. Pour some extra sugar into a shallow bowl, add the churros while still hot and toss well to coat. Repeat with the remaining dough and sugar to make about 15 churros.

To assemble the sundaes, generously drizzle dulce de leche around the sides and over the base of serving glasses. Dollop a little whipped cream in the bottom, top with a scoop of ice cream, then drizzle with dulce de leche. Repeat this layering, finishing with whipped cream and dulce de leche. Place the churros down the sides, then top with a couple of squares of chocolate and serve immediately.

CHURROS

canola oil, to deep-fry

25 g (1 oz) unsalted butter

1 tablespoon caster (superfine) sugar, plus extra to coat

pinch of fine salt

125 ml (4 fl oz/½ cup) water

75 g (2¾ oz/½ cup) plain (all-purpose) flour

1 egg

TIP *To make dulce de leche, remove the label from a tin of sweetened condensed milk, then place the unopened tin in a saucepan and cover completely with water. Cook over medium–high heat for 2 hours, topping up with water so the tin is completely covered at all times (or it may explode!). Cool completely, then open the tin to reveal the dulce de leche.*

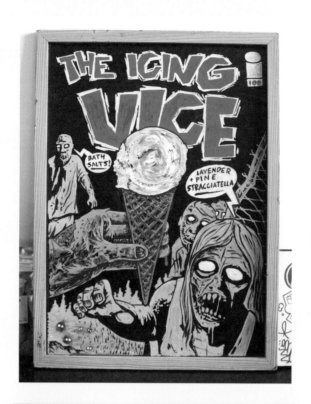

IPA hot chocolate & marshmallows

Forget the pallid hot chocolates of your past. The only sort you should ever drink should be thick, dark and rich. It's a maxim New York upholds with heart-racing cups found across town, from Maman's inventive take featuring dried lavender to Momofuku Milk Bar's marshmallow-topped approach.

For me, the king of hot chocs is undoubtedly The City Bakery's, which by some accounts uses up to 100 grams (3½ ounces) of the good stuff per cup. It's pretty much liquid chocolate, and every bit as good as that sounds. The iconic bakery celebrates its much-loved drink each February with daily-changing flavours and it's in this vein that I've made my own – with a twist of Brooklyn IPA craft beer, whose melange of fruity undertones plays off those also found in quality dark chocolate. It's also topped with an iceberg-size marshmallow, 'cause when you're going all out …

To make the marshmallows, grease and line a 22 cm (8¾ in) square baking tin with baking paper. Place the sugar, glucose and water in a saucepan over medium–high heat and stir until the sugar dissolves, then cook for a further 12–15 minutes or until it reaches 125°C (255°F). Meanwhile, soften the gelatine in a bowl of cold water for 5 minutes, then squeeze out the excess liquid. Remove the syrup from the heat, then whisk in the gelatine (be careful as it will bubble up). Using an electric mixer, whisk the egg whites to stiff peaks. Reduce the speed to low and, with the motor running, gradually add the hot syrup mixture until combined, then whisk for 5 minutes or until cool. Spread the marshmallow mixture over the prepared tin, smoothing the top, then refrigerate for 1–2 hours or until set.

Place a sheet of baking paper on a work surface. Combine the icing sugar and cornflour in a bowl, then sift half over the baking paper. Turn out the marshmallow onto the icing sugar mixture then, using a large sharp knife, cut into 20 pieces. Sift over the remaining icing sugar mixture and turn to coat all over, then transfer the marshmallows and any remaining icing sugar mixture to an airtight container. The marshmallows will keep at room temperature for 2–3 days.

When you are ready to make the hot chocolate, pour the milk and cream into a saucepan over medium heat and bring almost to the boil, then remove from the heat. Add the chocolate and sugar, stand for 3–5 minutes, then whisk until melted, well combined and dark. Add the IPA and whisk to combine.

Divide evenly among glasses and serve topped with marshmallows.

MAKES 4–6

500 ml (17 fl oz/2 cups) milk

500 ml (17 fl oz/2 cups) pouring (whipping/heavy) cream

350 g (12½ oz) dark chocolate (70% cocoa solids), finely chopped

75 g (2¾ oz/⅓ cup firmly packed) light brown sugar

160 ml (5½ fl oz/⅔ cup) Indian pale ale (IPA) (see tip)

MARSHMALLOWS

165 g (6 oz/¾ cup) caster (superfine) sugar

70 g (2½ oz) glucose syrup

100 ml (3½ fl oz) water

3 titanium-strength gelatine leaves

3 egg whites

35 g (1¼ oz/¼ cup) pure icing (confectioners') sugar

35 g (1¼ oz/¼ cup) cornflour (cornstarch)

TIP *Like most craft beers, every IPA (Indian pale ale) is different, so you may need to experiment before you hit upon the right one (you want a big, hoppy, bitter, citrusy one). You can add more beer to taste, but don't add more than an extra 1–2 tablespoons as it will change the consistency of the hot chocolate. Instead, try a different IPA.*

New York food markets

'Smorgasburg, the open-air market held every Saturday in an empty lot on a Williamsburg waterfront, is like a summer rock festival for food,' wrote The New York Times in a piece entitled The Woodstock of Eating, when Smorgasburg launched in 2011. On The Chew, Mario Batali called it 'the single greatest thing I've ever seen gastronomically in New York City'. Today, Smorgasburg attracts around 10,000 foodies each Saturday, and Sunday in Prospect Park, and other awesome outdoor food markets – Madison Square Eats (Flatiron; above), Broadway Bites (Midtown), Hester St Fair (LES) and Brooklyn Flea (Dumbo) – are now found across town.

Black Tap shake

Black Tap Craft Burgers & Beer's Instagram sensation. It blew up on social media, was picked up by TV, then went more viral.

MILKSHAKE BASICS + CONFECTIONERY BLING + A BUCKETLOAD OF SAUCE + A MOUNTAIN
OF CREAM + FOUR DIFFERENT FLAVOURS (LIKE SWEET 'N' SALTY)

Allow three hours to get your hands on one, plus 1600 calories.

The new ice-cream parlour

Morgenstern's Finest Ice Cream in Lower East Side epitomises the new American ice-cream parlour: old-school trimmings like swivel stools meets experimental flavours. It was all about coconut ash when I was there, but salted caramel pretzel is the long-time best seller and there's a collab each month with top chefs, such as Mario Batali. In summer, lines stretch out the door and the atmosphere is electric (which dulls the pain of waiting).

Sparkling blood orange sorbet float

On any given Saturday or Sunday, hungry hordes line up at chic cafes and restaurants for the cultural phenomenon that is New York brunch. It starts some time before noon and, fuelled by bottomless cocktails and coffee, often continues until dinner. Personally, I love it. It has the same energy as a concert, plus good food. And there are few things better than daytime drinking.

Quality Eats, Rider, High Street on Hudson and Freehold are among my favourite dine-in spots. But New Yorkers often play host to brunch at home and, inspired by their love of ice-cold floats, mimosas and new-favourite frosé (the fruity frozen rosé slushie that's stormed social media), this is what I would bring. An elegant mix of blood orange and basil sorbet drowned in sparkling wine, it's part drink, part dessert and very refreshing. It's also easy to make and, served in a champagne coupe, a showstopper.

Place the sugar and half of the orange juice in a small saucepan over medium–high heat and cook, stirring, until the sugar is dissolved. Transfer to a bowl with the basil and remaining juice, and stir to combine. Cover and refrigerate for 1 hour or until cold.

Strain the mixture through a fine sieve, discarding the solids. Churn in an ice-cream maker according to the manufacturer's instructions. Transfer to a container and freeze for 3 hours or until firm.

Place a scoop of sorbet in each champagne coupe, pour over some sparkling wine and serve immediately.

SERVES 6

220 g (8 oz/1 cup) caster (superfine) sugar

500 ml (17 fl oz/2 cups) blood orange juice

¼ large bunch of basil, leaves picked, torn

sparkling wine, to serve

SANTINA, CHELSEA
13.47

Hit list

Trucks, carts & market stands

La Newyorkina

240 SULLIVAN ST, NEW YORK (GREENWICH VILLAGE);
PLUS SEASONAL CARTS AROUND TOWN.

Fany Gerson, mastermind behind Dough doughnuts (see *Doughnuts*, page 58), also feeds New Yorkers' sweet appetite with Mexican popsicles known as paletas. Made with seasonal fruit and bursting with pure flavour, they're the city's best in my book. The first bricks and mortar La Newyorkina store was soon to open at the time of writing.

Melt Bakery

132 ORCHARD ST, NEW YORK (LES).

Eight downright tasty ice-cream sandwiches can be found in-store and in pushcarts dotted around the city. It's the cookies that separate them from their competitors, each bespoke for each ice-cream filling. I finished the Cinnamax – chewy snickerdoodles with Vietnamese cinnamon ice cream – in two minutes flat.

Mister Softee + New York Ice Cream

JUST ABOUT EVERYWHERE!

I shouldn't put these two together, particularly as they're engaged in a turf war with each other (seriously, there have been physical fist fights), but both soft-serve trucks are synonymous with the city. School kids go mad for them and, to my surprise, I really liked the creamy base and old-school toppings, too.

People's Pops

HIGH LINE; SMORGASBURG; AND BROOKLYN FLEA.

Seasonal fruit from NYC greenmarkets are used to make the refreshing range of popsicles and pure syrups poured over shaved-to-order ice. They go down a treat in the hot summer sun at a flea market or food fair, which is conveniently where their seasonal stands are located.

Ronnybrook Farm Dairy

UNION SQUARE GREENMARKET;
PLUS OTHER FARMERS' MARKETS.

Dairy from this local artisan producer is used by restaurants, ice-cream vendors and shake makers all over town, and you can buy it direct, as milk or yoghurt, at a handful of farmers' markets. The creamy chocolate milk tastes just like it used to.

The Good Batch

936 FULTON ST, BROOKLYN (CLINTON HILL);
PLUS MARKETS INCLUDING SMORGASBURG.

This Brooklyn bakery is best known for its delicious ice-cream sandwiches sold in-store and at weekend markets. There are around five in the range, including the Birthday Cake with funfetti sugar cookies, the Mint Brownie and, my pick, The Crispy with caramel rice krispies and vanilla ice cream.

Wowfulls

SMORGASBURG (WILLIAMSBURG AND PROSPECT PARK).

Hong Kong egg waffles, known as gai daan jai, may have been invented in the 1950s, but they look right at home in NYC. It could be the ice cream they cloak, the flavours from chocolate to matcha, and the OTT toppings. They go off on Instagram and are a hit at the outdoor food markets where they're found.

Ice creameries

10Below Ice Cream

132 ALLEN ST, NEW YORK (CHINATOWN);
PLUS THREE MORE LOCATIONS.

With hip hop pumping, this basement shop feels more like a club than an ice creamery. Then there's the Thai-style ice-cream rolls – liquid cream poured onto an ice-cold plate, then artfully spooled – which come with a spectrum of mix-ins and toppings, from matcha to scorched marshmallows.

Ample Hills Creamery

623 VANDERBILT AVE, BROOKLYN (PROSPECT HEIGHTS);
PLUS FIVE MORE LOCATIONS.

Where others drill down on single flavours, Ample Hills excels in combinations and texture, making it my favourite in New York City. The Munchies, for example, loads pretzel ice cream with Ritz, M&Ms and potato chips, and is so good I asked for the recipe (see page 152). Each location features an off-the-hook neighbourhood-inspired flavour, too.

Big Gay Ice Cream Shop

125 E 7TH ST, NEW YORK (EAST VILLAGE);
PLUS GREGARIOUS FOOD TRUCKS.

Using a proprietary ice-cream base from Ronnybook Dairy Farm and grown-up toppings, this is soft serve like you've never tried before. The hit cone Salty Pimp – vanilla soft serve injected with dulce de leche, sprinkled with sea salt and doused in chocolate – is my pick, but the Apple Gobbler sundae with apple butter sauce, bourbon butterscotch and graham cracker crumbs is just as awesome.

Brooklyn Farmacy & Soda Fountain

513 HENRY ST, BROOKLYN (CARROLL GARDENS).

The soda fountains and ice-cream parlours of yesteryear are brought to life in this immaculately restored original 1920s apothecary. Pull up a red twirling stool, order a float or New York egg cream and it's just like it used to be. With inventive sundaes topped with potato chips or fashioned after Twix chocolate bars, it's probably even better.

Davey's Ice Cream

137 1ST AVE, NEW YORK (EAST VILLAGE).

You'll find old-school styling with new-school flavours, including speculaas chocolate chip and the spectacular strong coffee, plus options from mega shakes to pies à la mode. It's all made on-site with artisan ingredients and by a cool bunch of rockabillys, too. Bring an appetite and order the epic split in a waffle banana boat.

Ice & Vice

221 E BROADWAY, NEW YORK (LES).

Creativity makes this another contender for New York's best ice cream. Among the more classic flavours is smoked dark chocolate and caramelised white choc ganache (aka Shade), while out-there options include Bath Salts with lavender and pine stracciatella. The perennially popular Tea Dance with nilgiri tea, lemon charcoal and salted caramel, served in a blue corn waffle cone, is ridiculously good.

Il laboratorio del gelato

188 LUDLOW ST, NEW YORK (LES).

It boasts over two hundred different gelato flavours and you can take your pick from around forty each day. Flavours scale the traditional (cassis, bourbon pecan, amaretto crunch) to the exotic (Turkish fig, kalamansi, pink peppercorn) and even extreme (wasabi, cheddar cheese).

Morgenstern's Finest Ice Cream

2 RIVINGTON ST, NEW YORK (LES).

Long before it starred in Aziz Ansari's cult show *Master of None*, the cool self-dubbed new American ice-cream parlour was pulling crowds for its slick retro fitout, spectacular flavours (go the salted pretzel and black coconut ash) and OTT sundaes, including an inspired take on Japanese honey toast and the five-scoop King Kong Banana Split.

OddFellows Ice Cream Co.

175 KENT AVE, BROOKLYN (WILLIAMSBURG);
75 E 4TH ST, NEW YORK (EAST VILLAGE).

It may look like a 1950s soda fountain, yet it's anything but old-fashioned. Ice creams range from burnt marshmallow (delectable) to red pepper fig, while popsicles are boozy and cones are decked in cotton candy. You can nab my favourite ice-cream sandwich – brioche just warmed in a sandwich press – at the Williamsburg flagship or head to the dedicated East Village Sandwich Shop.

Snowdays Shaved Cream Co.

241 E 10TH ST, NEW YORK (EAST VILLAGE);
167 7TH AVE S, NEW YORK (WEST VILLAGE);
37–20 PRINCE ST, QUEENS (FLUSHING).

Take Taiwanese shaved ice, substitute frozen cream and you get feather-light creamy ribbons known as shaved snow and the hottest Asian dessert trend. At Snowdays, the striking ice cream comes in homeland (roasted black sesame) to New York (cheesecake) flavours, with toppings to mix and match. The Yeti Tracks with blueberry and cookies 'n' cream is Insta famous.

The Original Chinatown Ice Cream Factory

65 BAYARD ST, NEW YORK (CHINATOWN).

This New York institution has been churning out ice cream for more than thirty years and still draws crowds for its creamy base and comprehensive range of Asian flavours, from red bean, pandan and taro, to don tot (egg custard), Chinese almond cookie and durian. A big thumbs up.

Van Leeuwen Artisan Ice Cream

620 MANHATTAN AVE, BROOKLYN (GREENPOINT);
48 E 7TH ST, NEW YORK (EAST VILLAGE);
PLUS 3 MORE LOCATIONS.

It began life as a food truck and now boasts five always-full New York stores. Purity defines these elegant ice creams, from the quality ingredients to the singular flavour. Earl grey is the best example, closely followed by mango yuzu. It's also praised for its vast vegan selection made with organic nut milks and pure cocoa butter.

OTHER NOTABLES: Cones, Grom Gelato, MilkMade Ice Cream, Sundaes and Cones, Mikey Likes It Ice Cream.

Bakeries, cafes & casual restaurants

Black Tap Craft Burgers & Beer

529 BROOME ST, NEW YORK (SOHO);
248 W 14TH ST, NEW YORK (MEATPACKING).

Images of the OTT milkshakes – one blinged out with chocolate pearls, lollipops and cotton candy, and all designed for Instagram fame – first appeared in early 2016 and queues at the casual restaurant have been insane ever since (allow a few hours). If you're after quality, you won't find it here, but even a sceptic like me was swept up in the fun.

Butter & Scotch

818 FRANKLIN AVE, BROOKLYN (CROWN HEIGHTS).

At this fabulous bakery-meets-bar, nothing escapes the kitchen without a dash of booze (see *Pies*, page 146), including the deliriously good drinks. Order The Nameshake with vanilla ice cream, butterscotch caramel and scotch, or the Pretty in Pink Float with Aperol, rosé and strawberry ice cream, and you'll never look at soda fountain drinks the same way again.

Dessert Club, ChikaLicious

204 E 10TH ST, NEW YORK (EAST VILLAGE).

Soft serve in a churros cone? That's right, and they get even better with Nutella-filled cores, salted caramel drizzle and sprinkles on top. Chikalicious is no stranger to dessert mash ups, with more delicious options including the Boston cream puff and dough'ssant (see *Pastries*, page 102).

Dominique Ansel Kitchen

137 7TH AVE S, NEW YORK (WEST VILLAGE).

The culinary mastermind has his finger in every pie, including soft serve, which he peddles over summer from the window counter at his mostly dine-in test kitchen. As expected, the flavours are inventive and sublime, including burrata ice cream with balsamic caramel and confit strawberry, and a special collab 'ice cream taco' with sweet corn ice cream in a masa waffle taco cone.

Mast

111 N 3RD ST, BROOKLYN (WILLIAMSBURG).

You can buy the progressive small-batch bean-to-bar chocolate all around New York (look for the cool packaging), but the beautiful flagship store is worth seeing in its own right. Join a tour of the production facility (there's one every hour) and there's a bevy of avant-garde drinks, including a cold-brew chocolate, too.

Momofuku Milk Bar

251 E 13TH ST, NEW YORK (EAST VILLAGE);
PLUS SIX MORE LOCATIONS.

What began as an idea for flavouring panna cotta is now the cult venue's signature and has spawned derivatives worldwide: cereal milk. The addictive cornflake-steeped milk is available in takeaway bottles, as delicious soft serve and shakes, as well as offshoot flavours including 'fruity' (Fruity Pebbles).

Serendipity 3

225 E 60TH ST, NEW YORK (UES).

Once frequented by the likes of Marilyn Monroe and Andy Warhol, these days the famed coffee shop feels more like a tourist trap. Press on; the legendary Frrrozen Hot Chocolate – somewhere between a slushy, iced chocolate and whipped cream mountain – is a little unrefined, but as good (and mammoth) as the rumours suggest.

Shake Shack

MADISON SQUARE PARK, MADISON AVE & E 23RD ST,
NEW YORK (FLATIRON); PLUS MORE LOCATIONS.

If it's not already, put New York's beloved homegrown chain on your list. Then, order a shake, float or cone to go with your burger and fries. Unlike other fast food operations, it uses real milk and no corn syrup. Even better are the Concretes, a delicious swirl of custard with chunky mix-ins, from Four & Twenty Blackbirds' pie to a Doughnut Plant doughnut.

The City Bakery

3 W 18TH ST, NEW YORK (FLATIRON).

While the exact ratio is a trade secret, it's believed this incredible hot chocolate (and twenty-five-year-old recipe) uses a luxurious 100 g (3½ oz)-plus dark chocolate per cup. Which explains why it'll set you back $8 – and why it's worth every cent. It's also blended to order, topped with an optional iceberg-sized marshmallow and downright dangerous with a pretzel croissant (see *Pastries*, page 103).

Restaurants

ABC Kitchen

35 E 18TH ST, NEW YORK (FLATIRON).

Celebrity chef Jean-Georges Vongerichten's casual-chic restaurant sticks to its seasonal manifesto with light fresh sweets. It deviates for a signature sundae: two scoops of salted caramel ice cream in a pool of hot fudge, whipped cream and candied popcorn and peanuts. Classic, indulgent and *very* good.

Lilia

567 UNION AVE, BROOKLYN (WILLIAMSBURG.)

Everyone's talking about this cool new Italian restaurant on an up-and-coming strip of Williamsburg, as well as its simple but incredible gelato soft serve. It's all about vanilla here, but you choose the topping, from chocolate shards to candied orange rind, and it comes out all pretty in a glass cup.

Marta

THE REDBURY HOTEL, 29 E 29TH ST, NEW YORK (MIDTOWN EAST).

Danny Meyer's mod pizzeria also dishes out top-notch frozen dolci, including seasonal gelati and sorbetti. I had the pleasure of trying the vivacious apple ginger moscato, and would put bets on the amarena cherry chip and Aperol spritz, too. It's equally known for its tiramisu ice-cream panino.

Narcissa

THE STANDARD EAST VILLAGE, 25 COOPER SQ, NEW YORK (EAST VILLAGE).

The classic ice-cream sundae is reimagined at this chic award-winning restaurant with refreshing olive oil ice cream, rich Meyer lemon curd and crunchy cherry biscotti. It's mature, original and heavenly, and a fixture on one of the best dessert menus in town (see *Plated*, page 233).

OTTO

1 5TH AVE, NEW YORK (WEST VILLAGE).

Mario Batali's popular pizzeria-enoteca is perhaps most famous for gelato. The signature olive oil, served as a striking coppetta (cup) with seasonal accoutrements including tangelo granita, pine nut brittle and candied cumquats, inspired chefs throughout the city with the combination, and is downright delizioso.

Parm

248 MULBERRY ST, NEW YORK (SOHO); PLUS THREE MORE LOCATIONS.

A classic American-Italian eatery seems like an unlikely home for sprinkles-topped ice-cream cakes, but start with the signature spumoni – layers of pistachio, strawberry and chocolate, and inspired by the traditional Italian dessert – and it quickly clicks in. Then, do as I did and tuck into another one, in twelve playful flavours, such as s'mores and pina colada.

Quality Eats

19 GREENWICH AVE, NEW YORK (WEST VILLAGE).

Dressed up scoops of ice cream are the signature at this West Village hotspot and boy are they fun: Birthday Cake topped with frosting and a candle, Bar Snacks with chocolate-coated potato chips, and This Shit is Bananas with candied bacon and cinnamon toast. The brunch breads are very good, too (see *Pastries*, page 103).

Plated & created

I heart NY

DAY 84, DESSERT 346: PRESERVED LEMON TART,
DIRTY FRENCH, LES

Before we even sat down, I loved this place with its
neon pink signage, sick background beats and antique
mirror splashed with melted black wax. Dirty French is
bistro meets punk-rock style and swagger. I ordered the
lemon meringue tart reworked with preserved lemon
to share with my mum, then pinched myself. Could this
city be any cooler?

Restaurants have been a particular pleasure, as much for
the out-of-this-world settings, vibe and dining experience
as the elevated approach to dessert. And if you skip
straight to the final course as we often did (just ask first
and dine off-peak), it's an affordable seat at establishments
of real repute.

Cake salons, mod patisseries and dessert bars are other
venues where dining, design and sweets are celebrated
together, and where you'll find dessert degustations,
desserts à la minute (made to order) and the most die-
hard sweet fans.

In New York, you can see, hear, smell, touch and taste
the experimentation, innovation and change, and you feel
like you're at the centre of the world. Social media is a
powerful way to experience the city from afar (it has also
brought about big, bad-ass desserts and sent sweet trends
viral), but being here, in real life, eating Dominque Ansel's
cookie shot or Cosme's husk meringue right where they
were created, is nothing short of exhilarating.

As the end of our adventure neared, I somehow scored a
table for two at Ralph Lauren's it-crowd, always-booked-
out Polo Bar. It's polished service, preppy decor, New York
perfection. Sure, the brownie à la mode is a simple affair,
but the whole experience? Unforgettable. New York has
been the secret ingredient this whole time, I realise. It is
just the right sweet finale.

«In New York, you can see, hear, smell, touch and taste the experimentation, innovation and change, and you feel like you're at the centre of the world.»

Pumpkin pie waffles

Another great thing about New York? Waffles. You can have them sweet or savoury, for breakfast, brunch, dinner and dessert, and in almost any style you fancy. Think buckwheat waffles with cinnamon butter at Pies 'n' Thighs. Or rosewater waffles with yoghurt and berries at Jack's Wife Freda. And waffles with buttermilk chicken and maple syrup, the great American classic, at Clinton St. Baking Company & Restaurant.

My New York pick could be the Liege, the crisp, caramelised Belgian beauty made with brioche dough and pearl sugar, and perfected at Wafels & Dinges, where they're slathered with your choice of speculaas spread, Nutella and more.

Another thing I love about waffles? They're a canvas for different flavours, like delicious pumpkin pie. Made with spiced pumpkin purée in the batter, which keeps them nice and moist, and topped with ice cream, candied pecans and salted caramel, these guys taste just like the autumn favourite in decadent waffle form. Better yet, you can prove the yeasted batter overnight in the fridge so it's ready come morning.

Combine the yeast and water in a large bowl and set aside for 5 minutes or until frothy, then whisk in the eggs, butter and vanilla until well combined. Sift over the flour, sugar and salt, and whisk until smooth. Cover with plastic wrap and set aside in a warm draught-free place for 1 hour or until doubled in size. (Alternatively, refrigerate overnight if making in advance.)

Meanwhile, to make the caramel sauce, place the sugar in a small saucepan over medium–high heat and cook, swirling the pan occasionally, for 7 minutes or until it becomes a caramel (make sure no lumps of sugar remain). Reduce the heat to low–medium, add the butter and whisk until combined, then gradually add the cream (be careful as it will bubble up) and salt, and whisk until smooth and combined. Remove from the heat and set aside to cool slightly.

Preheat the oven to 180°C (350°F) and line a baking tray with baking paper.

To make the candied pecans, place the sugar and water in a small saucepan over medium–high heat. Bring to a simmer, stirring until the sugar dissolves, then add the pecans and stir to coat. Transfer to the prepared tray and bake for 8 minutes or until caramelised and roasted. Cool, then roughly chop.

MAKES 10

1½ teaspoons dried yeast

80 ml (2½ fl oz/⅓ cup) lukewarm water

4 eggs

125 g (4½ oz) unsalted butter, melted, cooled

1 teaspoon natural vanilla extract

200 g (7 oz/1⅓ cups) plain (all-purpose) flour

1 tablespoon caster (superfine) sugar

¼ teaspoon fine salt

150 g (5½ oz/½ cup) tinned pumpkin purée (see tip)

¼ teaspoon freshly grated nutmeg

1 teaspoon ground cinnamon

½ teaspoon ground allspice

80 g (2¾ oz/½ cup) pearl sugar (see tip)

vanilla ice cream or whipped cream (or both!), to serve

SALTED CARAMEL SAUCE
110 g (4 oz/½ cup) caster
(superfine) sugar
30 g (1 oz) unsalted butter,
chopped
60 ml (2 fl oz/¼ cup) pouring
(whipping/heavy) cream
½ teaspoon sea salt flakes

CANDIED PECANS
55 g (2 oz/¼ cup) caster
(superfine) sugar
1½ tablespoons water
120 g (4½ oz/1 cup) pecans

When you are ready to cook the waffles, preheat your waffle iron or maker. Add the pumpkin purée and spices to the waffle batter and stir until well combined, then stir in the pearl sugar. Cook the waffles, in batches, until golden (the cooking time will depend on your waffle maker).

Scoop ice cream or dollop whipped cream generously over the waffles, then drizzle over the salted caramel sauce and scatter with candied pecans. Serve immediately.

TIPS *If you can't find tinned pumpkin purée or you'd prefer to make your own, microwave 200 g (7 oz) of butternut pumpkin (squash) flesh for 10 minutes or until tender. Drain and cool completely, then blend to a smooth purée. You'll need 150 g (5½ oz/½ cup) for the recipe.*

Pearl (or nib) sugar is hard, large granules of white sugar that don't melt at baking temperatures. It's readily available from speciality food shops. Coarsely crushed sugar cubes will produce a similar effect.

New York food halls

There's the older guard like Eataly and Chelsea Market, combining gourmet food products with smart-casual dining. Now there's the new wave with quick-service food in cool settings (the gourmet food court if you will). Think Hudson Eats and Union Fare. Basically, food halls are one of the biggest food trends to hit NYC in recent years, and you can now find them all around town. Here are a few more you gotta check out: Berg'n (Crown Heights), City Kitchen (Times Square), Gotham West Market (Hell's Kitchen), The Plaza Food Hall (Central Park South) and Urbanspace Vanderbilt (Midtown East).

The museum restaurant

*One rainy day, I had dessert at Untitled at The Whitney. The museum restaurant is
one of the best; the design is just so mod. I don't know if it was because I was alone,
pregnant, or because they love desserts as much as I do, but after my big slice of cake,
they brought me the cookie plate with warm milk on the house.*

Oatmeal cookie shots

Who doesn't like a cookie? New Yorkers *love* them. They grab them from bakeries, for sit downs in cafes and have them delivered to their homes in the wee hours.

You can even find cookies in the finest restaurants in town, served just like when you were a kid: warm from the oven with a glass of milk. Only much better, of course: baked to order with ingredients like Valrhona chocolate and burnt butter, and served with Tahitian vanilla-infused milk. It was one of the biggest trends when I visited, with highlights at Untitled and Upland.

The deconstructed take with cookie shards and milk ice at The NoMad is one of my favourite riffs on the theme, but the most famous is Dominique Ansel's legendary shot glass forged from a choc chip cookie and filled with warm milk. This is my rendition, made with another American classic, the oatmeal cookie, and every bit as good.

Sift the flour, cinnamon, bicarbonate of soda and salt into a bowl and set aside. Using an electric mixer, beat the butter and sugars for 1 minute or until light and creamy. Add the flour mixture and beat on low speed until just combined. Add the oats, eggs and vanilla, and beat until combined. Cover the bowl with plastic wrap and refrigerate for 1 hour or overnight.

Grease an eight-hole shot glass mould. Divide the dough in half and return one portion to the fridge. Roll out the remaining portion between two sheets of baking paper to a 3 cm (1¼ in) thick, 24 cm (9½ in) square (the size and thickness of the dough is very important for filling the moulds properly). Remove the top sheet of baking paper then, using a ruler and sharp knife, cut into eight 12 cm (4¾ in) × 6 cm (2½ in) rectangles. Transfer the dough on the baking paper to a tray and refrigerate for 30 minutes or until just firm.

Preheat the oven to 180°C (350°F).

Place a cookie dough rectangle inside each shot glass mould, ensuring the dough covers the bottom, is evenly spread throughout the mould and does not come above the rim (you may need to use your fingers to massage it around and down; if the dough is too stiff, allow it to soften slightly at room temperature). Place the moulds on a baking tray and bake for 25 minutes or until golden and crisp. Remove from the oven and if the cookie dough has puffed above the rim, gently press to flatten (this is the base of the shot glass, so if it's uneven it will topple). Cool the cookies in the mould, then refrigerate for 1 hour or until firm. Carefully unmould the cookies. Repeat with the remaining dough (or refrigerate for up to 2 days, or freeze for another time).

Using your finger, generously coat the inside of each cookie shot glass with melted chocolate, ensuring there are no holes. Refrigerate for 20 minutes or until set, then repeat the process. Serve chilled or at room temperature filled with milk.

MAKES 16

260 g (9 oz/1¾ cups) plain (all-purpose) flour

1 teaspoon ground cinnamon

1 teaspoon bicarbonate of soda (baking soda)

½ teaspoon fine salt

180 g (6½ oz) unsalted butter, chopped, softened

220 g (8 oz/1 cup firmly packed) light brown sugar

75 g (2¾ oz/⅓ cup) caster (superfine) sugar

180 g (6½ oz/2 cups) rolled (porridge) oats

2 eggs

1 teaspoon natural vanilla extract

150 g (5½ oz) white or dark chocolate, melted

warm milk, to serve

TIP *Silicone shot glass moulds are available from speciality kitchenware stores.*

THE STANDARD GRILL,
CHELSEA
11.07

Flatiron

Named after the triangle-shaped Flatiron Building. It was the world's first steel-frame
skyscraper and clad in white terracotta, but you'd never know it from its colour.

I was tempted every time I passed Shake Shack. It's the burgers, yes, but also
magical Madison Square Park (above).

Anonymous, *waiter*

*'I like chocolate everything – filled with chocolate, topped with chocolate
and dunked in chocolate. And especially chocolate cake.'*

Black & white lava cake

Like most New Yorkers, I find the black and white cookie – a sponge cake round covered in fondant – underwhelming. These days, only a handful of bakeries still bother to make the original.

But the sweet New York icon lives on in the city's countless inspired desserts, from Mah-Ze-Dahr's snickerdoodle and Amy's Bread's towering layer cake to the sundae at Russ & Daughters Cafe and OTTO's gelato coupe. Its appeal is understandably enduring – chocolate, vanilla and killer monochromatic looks.

The idea for my own black and white creation came to life one afternoon over Spot Dessert Bar's signature chocolate lava cake with a surprise green liquid matcha centre. Michel Bras first created the dessert in the 1980s with an oozy chocolate ganache core; here, it's luscious cream that theatrically spills out.

Place 60 ml (2 fl oz/¼ cup) of cream in the centre of a small piece of plastic wrap, then twist the edges to enclose into a ball. Repeat to make four balls in total, then freeze for 2 hours or until firm (the cream won't be frozen through).

Place the chocolate and butter in a heatproof bowl set over a saucepan of gently simmering water (don't let the bowl touch the water) and stir until melted and combined. Add the coffee and stir to combine, then remove from the heat and cool slightly. In a separate bowl, whisk the eggs and caster sugar until well combined, then whisk in the flour. Add the egg mixture to the chocolate mixture and whisk to combine.

Grease four 250 ml (8½ fl oz/1 cup) dariole moulds. Fill the moulds 1 cm (½ in) deep with chocolate batter. Unwrap the cream balls and place on top, then pour over the chocolate batter to cover (the batter will come almost to the top). Freeze for 3 hours or until firm.

Preheat the oven to 200°C (400°F).

Place the dariole moulds on a baking tray, then bake the cakes for 25 minutes or until the top is cooked and the edges are pulling away from the sides. (It's hard to tell visually when the cakes are perfectly cooked, but it's better to have them slightly over than under otherwise the cakes will collapse.) Cool for 5 minutes then, working quickly and carefully, invert the cakes out of the moulds into bowls. Dust with icing sugar and serve immediately with quenelles of stracciatella ice cream, if desired.

MAKES 4

240 ml (8 fl oz) double (extra-thick/clotted) cream

180 g (6½ oz) dark chocolate (70% cocoa solids), finely chopped

180 g (6½ oz) unsalted butter, chopped

1 teaspoon instant coffee granules dissolved in 2 teaspoons warm water

4 eggs

165 g (6 oz/¾ cup) caster (superfine) sugar

115 g (4 oz/¾ cup) plain (all-purpose) flour

pure icing (confectioners') sugar, to dust

stracciatella ice cream, to serve (optional)

TIP *You can also serve the cakes in the moulds. It's safer if you're not sure that they're adequately baked around the sides, and (almost) as showstopping.*

DEVOCION, WILLIAMSBURG
16.35

S'mores baked Alaska

Baked Alaska made a comeback in the 1990s, but hasn't been a Gotham favourite for a while now. Which is interesting given that Delmonico's, America's first fine-dining restaurant and a New York institution, is credited with importing it from France.

If baked Alaska reappears again, it should be in s'mores form! For me, the signature meringue and combination of hot and cold elements recalls all that is great about the fireside treat. I savoured incredible upmarket s'mores all across the city, from Dominique Ansel's famous frozen version that's torched to order to a standout interpretation at The Standard East Village's hot new restaurant Narcissa. But not one s'mores baked Alaska.

So I'm leading the charge. Here, a buttery cookie base is topped with molten chocolate cake, a scoop of the best coffee ice cream you can find, and finished off in charred sticky meringue. It's rich and *the most delicious* dessert.

Preheat the oven to 200°C (400°F). Grease six 150 ml (5 fl oz) ramekins and place on a baking tray.

Place the chocolate and butter in a heatproof bowl set over a saucepan of gently simmering water (don't let the bowl touch the water) and stir occasionally until melted and smooth. Set aside to cool.

Place the eggs, sugar, almond meal, flour and salt in a bowl and whisk until well combined. Add the chocolate mixture and stir until well combined, then divide evenly among the ramekins. Bake the cakes for 13 minutes or until the tops are just cooked (the cakes will be slightly gooey in the centre). Cool completely in the ramekins, then turn out and set aside until needed.

To make the butter cookies, sift the flour, bicarbonate of soda and baking powder into a bowl. Add the sugars and butter and, using an electric mixer, beat until the mixture clumps together. Shape into a disc, wrap in plastic wrap and refrigerate for 30 minutes.

Reduce the oven temperature to 180°C (350°F).

Roll out the dough between two sheets of baking paper to a rough 3 mm (⅛ in) thick, 25 cm (10 in) square. Transfer to a baking tray and remove the top sheet of baking paper, then bake for 8 minutes or until just golden and still soft. Remove from the oven. While still warm, using an 8.5 cm (3¼ in) cookie cutter (or a cutter slightly bigger than the cakes), cut out six rounds, then cool completely on the tray with the offcuts (you get to snack on these later!).

recipe continued »

MAKES 6

150 g (5½ oz) dark chocolate (55% cocoa solids), finely chopped

125 g (4½ oz) unsalted butter, chopped

3 eggs

110 g (4 oz/½ cup) caster (superfine) sugar

2 tablespoons almond meal

2 tablespoons plain (all-purpose) flour

¼ teaspoon fine salt

6 large scoops coffee ice cream

BUTTER COOKIES

115 g (4 oz/¾ cup) plain (all-purpose) flour

½ teaspoon bicarbonate of soda (baking soda)

½ teaspoon baking powder

1½ tablespoons caster (superfine) sugar

55 g (2 oz/¼ cup firmly packed) light brown sugar

90 g (3 oz) unsalted butter, chopped, softened

To make the marshmallow meringue, place all the ingredients in a large heatproof bowl set over a saucepan of gently simmering water (don't let the bowl touch the water). Cook, whisking, for 2 minutes or until the sugar is dissolved and the mixture is warm. Remove from the heat and, using an electric mixer, whisk for 5 minutes or until stiff peaks form and the mixture is cool.

Just before serving, fill a piping (icing) bag fitted with a 9 mm (½ in) plain nozzle with meringue. Divide the cookies among serving plates. If necessary, warm the chocolate cakes for 20 seconds in the microwave until just gooey in the centre but not warm, then place on top of the cookies. Using an ice cream scoop, place a generous scoop of ice cream on one cake. Working quickly, pipe buds of meringue all over to cover the ice cream, cake and base completely. (Alternatively, use a spatula to cover them freeform.) Repeat with the remaining cakes and meringue. Using a kitchen blowtorch, scorch the meringue, then serve immediately.

TIP *Make sure the ice cream is nice and hard or it will melt before you've finished assembling.*

MARSHMALLOW MERINGUE
8 egg whites
440 g (15½ oz/2 cups) caster (superfine) sugar
180 g (6½ oz/½ cup) glucose syrup

Rice pudding with ginger, caramel & sesame crumbs

If there's a city that can turn any sweet penchant into a craze, it's New York. Case in point: rice pudding. Before rainbow desserts, cronuts and cupcakes, the creamy comfort food once reserved for the home kitchen or ethnic purveyor took on new life in the hands of a New York local who opened Rice to Riches, the first store in the world dedicated to rice pudding. He modeled his store on the gelaterias of Italy, with rice pudding abundantly displayed in tempting flavours from rocky road to French toast, and the concept took off. Gotham's size means even niche persuasions start with a strong following.

This upmarket take, with an undertone of fresh ginger and decadently covered in dark caramel and sesame crumb, is an elegant ode to the rustic treat now immortalised in the rice pudding emporiums of New York and around the globe. Served in glasses, it's equal parts comfort food and chic, and can be prepared ahead of time and rewarmed just before serving.

Place the milk, cream, sugar, lemon zest, cinnamon and ginger in a saucepan over medium–high heat and bring almost to the boil, stirring to dissolve the sugar. Add the rice and stir to combine, then reduce the heat to low–medium and cook, stirring occasionally, for 35 minutes or until the rice is tender and the mixture is thickened. Cool slightly, then stir in the egg yolk until well combined.

Meanwhile, preheat the oven to 180°C (350°F) and line a baking tray with baking paper.

To make the sesame crumb, combine the flour, sugar and sesame seeds in a bowl. Add the butter and, using your fingers, rub it into the flour mixture until a dough forms. Spread over the prepared tray and bake for 16 minutes or until golden and crisp. Cool completely, then break into crumbs.

To make the burnt caramel, place the sugar and water in a saucepan over medium–high heat and bring to the boil, stirring until the sugar dissolves. Cook, without stirring, for 10 minutes or until it becomes a dark caramel. Remove from the heat. Gradually add the cream (be careful as the mixture will bubble and spit) and stir until smooth.

Divide the rice pudding among four 200 ml (7 fl oz) serving glasses. Pour over the caramel and scatter with the sesame crumb. Serve warm or at room temperature.

MAKES 4

875 ml (29½ fl oz/3½ cups) milk

125 ml (4 fl oz/½ cup) pouring (whipping/heavy) cream

110 g (4 oz/½ cup) caster (superfine) sugar

finely grated zest of 1 lemon

1 cinnamon stick

8 cm (3½ in) piece fresh ginger, peeled, cut into 2 cm (¾ in) pieces

150 g (5½ oz/¾ cup) long-grain white rice, rinsed under cold water

2 egg yolks, lightly beaten

SESAME CRUMB

50 g (1¾ oz/⅓ cup) plain (all-purpose) flour

55 g (2 oz/¼ cup) caster (superfine) sugar

1 teaspoon sesame seeds, toasted

50 g (1¾ oz) unsalted butter, chopped, softened

BURNT CARAMEL

110 g (4 oz/½ cup) caster (superfine) sugar

60 ml (2 fl oz/¼ cup) water

60 ml (2 fl oz/¼ cup) pouring (whipping/heavy) cream

Milk & honey

The NoMad Restaurant's riff on milk and cookies. Finally, a deconstructed dessert that delivers.

MILK ICE + HONEY-OATMEAL CRUMBLE + HONEY BRITTLE + DEHYDRATED MILK FOAM + BUCKWHEAT HONEY

As a kid, chef Daniel Humm drank a glass of warm milk with honey every night before bed, so the inspiration goes …

NoMad

*Short for North of Madison Square. It didn't have a name until the late noughts
'cause there wasn't much here. Now it's on-trend.*

*At Upland, I'd order the signature burger (top five in the city), then sample
a different dessert each time (the menu is always changing).*

Midtown

It's the most iconic neighbourhood, but very touristy and congested. In saying that, there are wonderful little pockets of serenity if you stop and look.

The view from the top of the Empire State Building is breathtaking, but I think Rockefeller's is fractionally better; you can see all of Central Park.

Bibble & Sip feels like a neighbourhood cafe even though it's in the heart of the CBD. People tend to linger here.

Meringue with Frederick Aquino, The Standard hotels

KEEP IT CLEAN

Make sure everything is clean and without a trace of oil; this means no little flecks of egg yolk in your egg whites, too.

OLDIE, BUT A GOODIE

The best whip will always be with egg whites that are a couple of days old and have been sitting at room temperature for a few hours.

THE SECRET TOUCH

Using cream of tartar helps stabilise egg whites and also gets rid of anything that might be left behind, such as oil.

EASY DOES IT

Always use caster (superfine) sugar instead of white (granulated), and whisk egg whites to soft peaks before gradually adding the sugar. Same goes for sugar syrup in Italian meringue.

Red velvet vacherin

Rainbow desserts may be all the rage, but red velvet is the OG of bright-coloured sweets. It's a fact not lost in New York, where there's a certain reverence for the American bakeshop classic.

For me, Magnolia Bakery's towering layer cake, Ample Hills' cream cheese ice cream with red velvet sponge, and Sweet Revenge cupcakes with berry coulis are its best traditional and new-school iterations.

This red velvet vacherin – striking red and white layers of meringue, cheesecake ice cream and raspberry sorbet – is my elegant homage to the original. It's, dare I say it, even better, and further proof that red velvet still rules.

To make the cheesecake ice cream, process all the ingredients in a food processor until smooth. Churn in an ice-cream maker according to the manufacturer's instructions, then transfer to an airtight container and freeze for 4 hours or until frozen.

To make the raspberry sorbet, place the sugar, glucose and water in a small saucepan over medium–high heat. Bring to the boil, stirring until the sugar dissolves, then leave to cool completely. Process the raspberries, lemon juice and syrup in a food processor to a smooth purée, then pass through a fine sieve, discarding the seeds. Churn in an ice-cream maker according to the manufacturer's instructions, then transfer to an airtight container and freeze for 3 hours or until frozen.

Preheat the oven to 120°C (235°F).

Using an electric mixer, whisk the egg whites and salt until soft peaks form. Whisking constantly, gradually add the caster sugar and whisk to stiff peaks. Sift over the icing sugar and cornflour, then fold to combine. Divide the mixture in half. Sift the cocoa over one portion and fold to combine, then fold in the food colouring.

Using a pencil, draw two 20 cm (8 in) × 10 cm (4 in) rectangles each on two sheets of baking paper (four rectangles in total), then place, pencil side down, on two baking trays. Using the templates as a guide, spread the white meringue over two rectangles, smoothing the tops. Spread the red meringue over the other two rectangles. Bake, swapping the trays halfway through, for 1 hour or until crisp but not coloured. Cool completely on the trays. The meringue will keep in an airtight container for 1 week.

To assemble, remove the ice cream and sorbet from the freezer to soften slightly. Meanwhile, line a 20 cm (8 in) × 10 cm (4 in) loaf tin with plastic wrap, allowing plenty of overhang, and place a layer of white meringue in the base (carefully trim the edges if necessary). Spread over half the ice cream and smooth the surface, then top with a layer of red meringue. Spread over the sorbet and top with the remaining piece of red meringue. Spread over the remaining ice cream, then finish, uneven edge up, with the remaining layer of white meringue (the vacherin will come up over the rim). Fold over the plastic wrap and freeze overnight so the meringue softens slightly.

To serve, carefully unmould the vacherin. Using a warm sharp knife, cut into 3 cm (1¼ in) thick slices and serve immediately with fresh raspberries, if desired.

SERVES 6–8

2 egg whites
pinch of fine salt
75 g (2¾ oz/⅓ cup) caster (superfine) sugar
75 g (2¾ oz/½ cup) pure icing (confectioners') sugar
1 tablespoon cornflour (cornstarch)
¾ teaspoon unsweetened (Dutch) cocoa powder
1 teaspoon red food colouring
fresh raspberries, to serve (optional)

CHEESECAKE ICE CREAM
200 g (7 oz) cream cheese, chopped, softened
180 ml (6 fl oz/¾ cup) pouring (whipping/heavy) cream
180 ml (6 fl oz/¾ cup) milk
165 g (6 oz/¾ cup) caster (superfine) sugar
pinch of fine salt

RASPBERRY SORBET
110 g (4 oz/½ cup) caster (superfine) sugar
1 tablespoon glucose syrup
60 ml (2 fl oz/¼ cup) water
300 g (10½ oz) fresh or frozen (thawed) raspberries
juice of ½ lemon

Union Square

Whenever I got off at Union Square station, I considered quickly ducking into Breads Bakery for a warm chocolate rugelach (and usually did).

At one end of Union Square Park is the greenmarket (above); at the other, skateboarders, musicians and activists, so it's always lively.

I avoided the mayhem of Soho and Midtown, and shopped the strip along Fifth Ave instead.

The dessert bar

New York has a few dedicated dessert bars and the appetites you'll find there make for great watching. At Spot Dessert Bar, plated desserts are sold individually, but most opt for the 'tapas' selection of three or more. Often it's groups of friends sharing, but equally it's petite girls or couples who down them without batting an eyelid.

Cosme's corn husk meringue with corn mousse

Epicurious called it 'basically The Most Instagrammed Dish of 2015'. *Eater* praised the 'Mexican pavlova', as did just about every review. When I finally tried the corn husk meringue with corn mousse at Cosme, superstar Mexican chef Enrique Olvera's lauded restaurant, I *had* to have the recipe for this otherworldly dessert.

Chef de cuisine Daniela Soto-Innes, who created it with Olvera and gladly granted my request, said it was inspired by her childhood in Mexico City. 'When my mum saw me carrying a bag of meringues filled with whipped cream, she knew my dad had been late picking up my sisters and me from school. She'd feel bad too and would make our favourite sweet corn soup.' I love desserts rooted in time and place, and this one with charred husks and burnt vanilla is spectacular.

Preheat the oven to 230°C (450°F).

Place the corn husks on a baking tray and bake, turning regularly, for 8–10 minutes or until dark brown and very dry. Cool and break into small pieces, then finely grind, in batches, in a spice grinder. Sift through a fine sieve; you should have 10 g (¼ oz) of husk powder.

Reduce the oven temperature to 90°C (195°F) and line a baking tray with baking paper.

Using an electric mixer, whisk the egg whites to soft peaks. With the motor running, gradually add the sugar and whisk to medium peaks. Add half the husk powder and whisk until stiff peaks form. Transfer to a piping (icing) bag fitted with a 1.5 cm (½ in) plain nozzle and pipe six 7 cm (2¾ in) rounds on the prepared tray. Bake for 1 hour or until the meringues are set and sound hollow when tapped on the bottom. Set aside for 2 hours or until completely cool.

Meanwhile, to make the corn mousse, place the corn kernels, sugar, salt and 180 ml (6 fl oz/¾ cup) cream in a saucepan over medium heat. Bring almost to the boil, then cook, stirring occasionally, for 5 minutes or until the corn is tender. Transfer to a food processor and process to a purée. Strain through a fine sieve, pressing the solids to extract as much liquid as possible. Discard the solids. Cool the purée completely, then whisk in the mascarpone. Using an electric mixer, whisk the remaining 80 ml (2½ fl oz/⅓ cup) cream until stiff peaks form, then fold into the mascarpone mixture. Cover and refrigerate until needed.

To make the burnt vanilla cream, cut the vanilla bean in half widthways. Roughly chop one half and place in a small saucepan. Cook, tossing occasionally, for 3–5 minutes or until fragrant. Cool, then finely grind in a spice grinder. Split the remaining half of the vanilla bean lengthways and scrape out the seeds. Using an electric mixer, whisk the cream, sugar, vanilla seeds and vanilla powder until stiff peaks form.

To assemble, divide the meringues among six plates. Using the back of a spoon, gently crack them open. Spoon over the vanilla cream and then the corn mousse. Sprinkle with the remaining husk powder and serve immediately.

MAKES 6

husks of 2 corn cobs, silks removed (reserve the corn for the mousse)
3 egg whites
180 g (6½ oz) caster (superfine) sugar

CORN MOUSSE
250 g (9 oz/1½ cups) corn kernels (from about 2 corn cobs)
1 tablespoon caster (superfine) sugar
⅛ teaspoon fine salt
260 ml (9 fl oz) pouring (whipping/heavy) cream
125 g (4½ oz/½ cup) mascarpone

BURNT VANILLA CREAM
1 vanilla bean
375 ml (12½ fl oz/1½ cups) thickened (whipping) cream
2 tablespoons pure icing (confectioners') sugar, sifted

Gramercy Tavern's strawberries & cream with sorrel ice

If there was a dessert that summed up New York right now, it would be Gramercy Tavern's strawberries and cream. It's seasonal (available only in summer), produce-driven (inspired by Tristar strawberries) and local (champions New York state dairy), nostalgic (it's strawberries and cream), updated (with angel food cake croutons) and inventive (plus sorrel ice). It's also seriously Instagramable (it looks like a lush forest floor).

It's not by chance that this exquisite dish exudes the spirit of the city; Danny Meyer's Gramercy Tavern, which has been going for over twenty years now, is synonymous with New York. Pastry chef Miro Uskokovic, who also oversees the much-loved desserts at Untitled at The Whitney and kindly shared his recipe with me, is among the best in town, too.

Incredible looks aside, this is a simple dessert at heart, which means quality ingredients make all the difference. Miro recommends the best sweet strawberries, fresh sorrel and artisan cream, cream cheese and crème fraîche you can find.

To make the sorrel ice, place the sugar and 80 ml (2½ fl oz/⅓ cup) of the water in a saucepan and bring to the boil, stirring to dissolve the sugar. Remove from the heat. Place the sugar syrup, sorrel leaves, lemon juice and the remaining water in a blender and blend until smooth. Pass through a fine strainer, pressing the solids to extract all the liquid, then discard the solids. Transfer to a shallow container and freeze overnight.

To make the angel food cake croutons, position an oven rack on the bottom shelf of the oven, then preheat the oven to 160°C (325°F). Set an angel food cake tin aside (do not grease it).

Using an electric mixer, whisk the egg whites, salt, lemon juice and vanilla on medium speed until frothy. Whisking constantly, gradually add the icing sugar until combined, then whisk until stiff peaks form. Fold in the flour in batches. Transfer the batter to the angel food cake tin, smooth the top and bake for 50 minutes or until a toothpick inserted in the centre comes out clean. Remove from the oven, then immediately invert the tin and place the central tube over an upturned funnel (some tins have feet to keep it elevated). Leave the cake inverted to cool completely before removing the tin.

Preheat the oven to 90°C (195°F) and line two baking trays with baking paper. Cut the cake into quarters and trim off all the browned edges, then tear the white cake centre into 1 cm (½ in) pieces. Spread in a single layer over the prepared trays and cook, swapping the trays halfway through, for 2½ hours or until the croutons are dry and crunchy (at Gramercy Tavern, they use a dehydrator, which retains the cake's white colour, but these croutons may become golden). Store in an airtight container until needed.

recipe continued »

SERVES 10–12

600 g (1 lb 5 oz) Tristar or other strawberries, hulled and quartered

micro marigold flowers, to serve (optional)

SORREL ICE
75 g (2¾ oz/⅓ cup) caster (superfine) sugar

760 ml (25½ fl oz/3 cups) water

160 g (5½ oz/4 cups firmly packed) sorrel leaves, plus extra to serve

3 teaspoons lemon juice

ANGEL FOOD CAKE CROUTONS
12 egg whites

½ teaspoon fine salt

2 teaspoons lemon juice

½ teaspoon natural vanilla extract

335 g (12 oz/2¼ cups) pure icing (confectioners') sugar, sifted

150 g (5½ oz/1 cup) cake or plain (all-purpose) flour, sifted

To make the strawberry jam, place the strawberries, sugar, vanilla and salt in a saucepan and cook, stirring, over medium heat for 15 minutes or until the strawberries break down and the juices are thickened. Remove from the heat and cool. Transfer to a blender with the lemon juice and blend until smooth.

To make the whipped cheesecake, using an electric mixer, beat the cream cheese until smooth. Add the remaining ingredients and whisk until stiff peaks form.

To assemble, toss the quartered strawberries with just enough strawberry jam to ensure the strawberries are well coated and sticky (you will have jam left over). Using a fork, scrape the sorrel ice to make ice crystals. Place a large dollop of whipped cheesecake in the centre of each serving plate, then surround with the strawberry mixture. Top with sorrel ice, then scatter over some angel food cake croutons, extra sorrel leaves and flowers, if desired. Serve immediately.

TIP *If you're not feeding a crowd, you can halve the recipes for the sorrel ice, whipped cheesecake, strawberry jam and strawberries, and save the remaining croutons for another time (or just eat them – they're so moreish).*

STRAWBERRY JAM

400 g (14 oz) Tristar or other strawberries, hulled and halved

150 g (5½ oz/⅔ cup) caster (superfine) sugar

½ teaspoon natural vanilla extract

¼ teaspoon fine salt

3 teaspoons lemon juice

WHIPPED CHEESECAKE

400 g (14 oz) cream cheese, chopped, softened

200 g (7 oz) crème fraîche (or sour cream)

200 ml (7 fl oz) thickened (whipping) cream

160 ml (5½ fl oz/⅔ cup) sweetened condensed milk

55 g (2 oz/¼ cup) caster (superfine) sugar

½ teaspoon natural vanilla extract

¼ teaspoon fine salt

Buttermilk panna cotta

In spite of all the pre-trip research, some of my most memorable dessert experiences were unplanned. Take Four & Twenty Blackbirds, where I'd tried every exquisite flavour on my list when the owners slipped me an unassuming slice of buttermilk chess pie. It became an all-time favourite.

Or Vinegar Hill House in Brooklyn's Vinegar Hill (New York neighbourhoods have the best names), after a cancelled reservation elsewhere led us to the rustic, produce-driven restaurant and a simple but sensational dessert: silky buttermilk custard with apple and buckwheat.

Buttermilk is far from exotic and is used in everything from pancakes to cakes, but it was an adventure in New York that made me appreciate and celebrate this everyday ingredient. Served in bowls, this just-set panna cotta is so easy and seriously luscious. Paired with seasonal fruit, such as poached nectarine, sliced mango or pomegranate seeds, it's also just the thing for a supper in Brooklyn, where simple, quality ingredients are often seen as stars.

Place the cream and sugar in a small saucepan over medium heat and bring almost to the boil, stirring to dissolve the sugar. Remove from the heat. Meanwhile, soften the gelatine in a bowl of cold water for 5 minutes. Drain and squeeze out any excess liquid. Add the gelatine to the cream mixture and whisk until melted and combined. Add the buttermilk and whisk until well combined, then divide among four 250 ml (8½ fl oz/1 cup) or six 150 ml (5 fl oz) serving bowls. Cover with plastic wrap and refrigerate overnight to set.

Serve the panna cotta with your choice of fruit.

MAKES 4–6

180 ml (6 fl oz/¾ cup) pouring (whipping/heavy) cream

165 g (6 oz/¾ cup) caster (superfine) sugar

3 gold-strength gelatine leaves

600 ml (20½ fl oz) buttermilk

fresh or poached seasonal fruit, to serve

HIGH LINE,
CHELSEA

15.13

UWS

Short for Upper West Side. It's a cultural, intellectual and residential neighbourhood, and one of Manhattan's biggest.

I could never leave the UWS without grabbing a bag of warm cookies from Levain Bakery, even if I had to line up for over an hour. They are just so damn good.

You can watch the ballet, opera or orchestra at the Lincoln Centre (above). Whatever you do, just go; the acoustics and setting are phenomenal.

UES

More commonly known as Upper East Side. Or New York's old money. It's pretty exclusive up there.

On Museum Mile, my favourite is the Metropolitan Museum of Art. The Guggenheim is a great building, but the collection is usually too abstract for me.

Two Little Red Hens make the best Brooklyn blackout cake. They don't sell it by the slice, so I used to buy a small cake and end up eating it all.

BRYANT PARK
16.32

Hit List

Bakeries, patisseries & cafes

Dominique Ansel Bakery

189 SPRING ST, NEW YORK (SOHO).

The cronut is undeniably the celebrity chef's most famous invention (see *Pastries*, page 102), but there are a number of other wild creations vying for second place. Frozen S'mores – chewy Turkish-style vanilla ice cream enveloped in marshmallow and torched to order – for one, and the glass-shaped chocolate chip cookie filled with vanilla-infused milk, aka Cookie Shot (available after 3 pm).

Dominique Ansel Kitchen

137 7TH AVE S, NEW YORK (WEST VILLAGE).

At his shinier cronut-free offshoot, the hybrid king also reworks the idea of a traditional bakery, serving many of the inventive sweets such as matcha beignets à la minute (made to order) for optimum enjoyment. He takes the dine-in concept even further in the upstairs dining room (dubbed UP for Unlimited Possibilities) with a ticketed after-hours seven-course tasting menu. (See also *Ice Cream*, page 186.)

Wafels & Dinges

15 AVENUE B, NEW YORK (ALPHABET CITY); PLUS MORE STOREFRONT AND FOOD TRUCK LOCATIONS.

Belgian waffles are the name of the game at this perennially popular purveyor that began life as a food truck. They're also spectacular, from the classic yeast-leavened Brussels to my favourite, the Liege, with traditional pearl sugar, and finished off with OTT 'dinges' (aka toppings), such as dulce de leche and Nutella.

Dessert bars

ChikaLicious Dessert Bar

203 E 10TH ST, NEW YORK (EAST VILLAGE).

Where few dessert bars stand the test of time, this one has been drawing crowds for over ten years. It's the chicer, degustation-only sister to Dessert Club Chikalicious across the road, and at just $16 for three courses – amuse bouche, dessert 'main' and petit fours – is a heck of a steal. The menu changes daily, bar the ethereal all-white fromage blanc cheesecake on a throne on ice.

Patisserie Tomoko

568 UNION AVE, BROOKLYN (WILLIAMSBURG).

Japanese reverence (and reinvention) of classic French patisserie is once again the focus of this elegant dessert bar on an up-and-coming strip of Williamsburg. Matcha, yuzu and black sesame are all on the roll call of owner-chef Tomoko Kato's three-course tasting menu and tea service, and set the tone in the takeaway cabinet, too.

Spot Dessert Bar

13 AND 5 ST MARKS PLACE, NEW YORK (EAST VILLAGE);
11 W 32ND ST, NEW YORK (KOREATOWN).

On any given day, local dessert lovers pack out this delicious dine-in dessert bar and order the 'tapas' set with three stunning plated desserts for $25. Signatures include the chocolate lava cake with its striking green matcha core and The Harvest, soft cheesecake hidden under chocolate soil in a matching terracotta pot.

Restaurants

Cosme

35 E 21ST ST, NEW YORK (FLATIRON).

To date, my favourite restaurant in the city. I won't luxuriate on global culinary star Enrique Olvera's contemporary Mexican menu (exquisite), the service (without a fault) or the dining room (understated cool), but they all play a role in the final note: corn husk meringue with corn mousse. The much talked about dessert is inventive yet familiar (a quasi Mexican pavlova), more savoury than sweet, and like nothing I've tried before. So of course I asked for the recipe – see page 220.

Craft

43 E 19TH ST, NEW YORK (FLATIRON).

While the dessert line up at Tom Colicchio's gilded fine-dining icon changes often, French and American classics with thoughtfully executed twists are a constant. Peach tarte tatin, for example, is served with chocolate pink peppercorn ice cream, while a large Parisian-style macaron is reinvented with a chocolate cheesecake core.

David Burke fabrick

ARCHER HOTEL, 47 W 38ᵀᴴ ST, NEW YORK (MIDTOWN).

This midtown restaurant is no stranger to theatrical desserts. When I was in town, it was the Big Apple tart complete with an NYC skyline-shaped cookie and a s'mores napoleon for two served with a mini cleaver. Thanksgiving saw the arrival of something even wilder: piecaken. Think pumpkin and pecan pies stuffed into a spiced pound cake, and topped with apple pie. Yes, a dessert version of the turducken.

Gramercy Tavern

42 E 20ᵀᴴ ST, NEW YORK (GRAMERCY).

Eating at Danny Meyer's iconic Gramercy Tavern is a New York experience, and you can choose from the more formal Dining Room or diffusion-label Tavern for a taste of Miro Uskokovic's special desserts. Upfront, childhood favourites, such as sundaes, floats and pie, are reimagined with restaurant flourishes, while the dining room explores ingredients, including the 'Strawberry' that was just so special I asked for the recipe – see page 222.

il Buco

47 BOND ST, NEW YORK (NOHO).

I'm not generally a fan of panna cotta, but the signature at this Mediterranean Noho haven – it's been on the menu for over twenty years – is panna cotta perfection: silky, light and just set. It's also drizzled with ten-year aged balsamic for an unusual and sophisticated twist.

Marta

29 E 29ᵀᴴ ST, NEW YORK (MIDTOWN EAST).

On top of frozen sweets (see *Ice Cream*, page 187), the Roman pizzeria in Midtown's Redbury Hotel is known for its sweet Italian classic remakes, including a cannoli cheesecake studded with chocolate chips and dripping with pistachio crema, and an ice-cream sandwich, which changes form each season.

Narcissa

THE STANDARD EAST VILLAGE, 25 COOPER SQ, NEW YORK (EAST VILLAGE).

Some of my most memorable restaurant desserts are found at this award-winner in the cool The Standard East Village hotel. The sophisticated sundae is a mainstay (see *Ice Cream*, page 187), while a warm flourless chocolate cake topped with charred meringue – their upmarket rendition of a s'more – just about blew my mind. They're also a steal at $10 a pop.

Per Se

TIME WARNER CENTER, 10 COLUMBUS CIRCLE, NEW YORK (MIDTOWN WEST).

You can savour Thomas Keller's sweet selection at Bouchon Bakery, and even a few plated desserts at the adjoining cafe, but the five-course dessert tasting at his fine-dining beacon Per Se is truly one of a kind. It's hosted in The Salon, where it's first come first serve, so arrive early.

Russ & Daughters Cafe

127 ORCHARD ST, NEW YORK (LES).

The restaurant offshoot to Russ & Daughters, the hundred-plus-year-old Jewish deli, is worth a visit for the art deco styling and effortlessly cool vibe. Then there's the take on traditional sweets: challah bread pudding, halva topped sesame ice cream (by day), and babka ice-cream sandwich and black and white cookie sundae (by night).

The Breslin

16 W 29ᵀᴴ ST, NEW YORK (MIDTOWN).

Star chef April Bloomfield also knocks out mean desserts across her six character-filled restaurants, including The Spotted Pig's banoffee and Salvation Burger's banana cream pies. The Breslin houses her widest selection, from s'mores brownie to peanut butter pudding, and ace pastries for brunch.

The NoMad Restaurant

THE NOMAD HOTEL, 1170 BROADWAY, NEW YORK (NOMAD).

Opt for a seat in the light-drenched atrium, then order the Milk and Honey: honey oat shortbread, honey brittle, dehydrated milk foam, milk ice and buckwheat honey. Finally, a deconstructed dessert that delivers (see page 212). Chef Daniel Humm of Eleven Madison Park acclaim is also behind the restaurant-bar's famed cookies and cream balls.

Index

Thank you

Writing this book would not have been possible without the following people. I can't thank you enough.

To my wonderful husband Steve, who backed the wild idea, uprooted our family for a season in New York, and supported me through the months of writing. Inés, my darling daughter, who helped me taste test, recipe test and gave up time with her mama so I could work. To Alejo, my little boy and constant companion, who trooped around the city while I was pregnant, and when he was three months old, and was nothing short of a dream baby. My mum Ruby, who babysat for I don't know how many days, also flew to New York to help out, and was my harshest and most helpful critic. My dad John, for giving up all that time with her. To my brother Terry and his girlfriend Krista, for madly letting two adults and two kids crash at their place for over a quarter of the year, and making New York feel like home. To Linda and Derek, my parents in law, who bravely looked after a toddler for over a month straight. And my best friend Mel, who also flew to New York to play nanny (and drink wine with me).

To Jane Willson, my incredible publisher, for loving the idea from day one and batting for me all the way. Loran McDougall, my editor, for supporting me so wonderfully through the process, and Rachel Carter, for her fantastic edit. To Andy Warren and Mark Campbell for the awesome design, Alicia Taylor, Deb Kaloper and Mimi Baines for the delectable photos, Averie Cole for the sweet pics of me, and all the other good folks at Hardie Grant and elsewhere who helped bring this beautiful book to life.

To New York's fantastic pastry chefs, bakers, ice-cream makers and more, for turning out the most delicious desserts. And these people in particular, who graciously gave their time, brains trust and sweet recipes: Brian Smith and Jackie Cuscuna (Ample Hills Creamery), Roger Gural (Arcade Bakery), Matt Lewis and Renato Poliafito (Baked), Allison Kave and Keavy Landreth (Butter & Scotch), Daniela Soto-Innes and Enrique Olvera (Cosme), Fany Gerson (Dough), Emily and Melissa Elsen (Four & Twenty Blackbirds), Miro Uskokovic (Gramercy Tavern), Jennifer Yee (Lafayette Grand Cafe & Bakery), Maury Rubin (The City Bakery) and Frederick Aquino (The Standard). You guys rock!

I'd also like to thank my body for not crumbling under all the desserts I ate this year. I promise I'll take better care of you (until next time).

And lastly, to New York, for being the number one city in the world.

Yasmin x

Published in 2017 by Hardie Grant Books, an imprint of
Hardie Grant Publishing

Hardie Grant Books (Melbourne)
Building 1, 658 Church Street
Richmond, Victoria 3121
hardiegrantbooks.com.au

Hardie Grant Books (London)
5th & 6th Floors
52–54 Southwark Street
London SE1 1UN
hardiegrantbooks.co.uk

Map (18–9) Knut Hebstreit/Shutterstock.com

A Cataloguing-in-Publication entry is available from the catalogue of the
National Library of Australia at www.nla.gov.au

The Desserts of New York
978 1 74379 212 4

Publishing Director: Jane Willson
Managing Editor: Marg Bowman
Project Editor: Loran McDougall
Editor: Rachel Carter
Design Manager: Mark Campbell
Designer: Andy Warren
Photographer (location): Yasmin Newman
Photographer (studio): Alicia Taylor
Stylist: Deborah Kaloper
Home Economist: Mimi Baines
Production Manager: Todd Rechner
Production Coordinator: Rebecca Bryson

Colour reproduction by Splitting Image Colour Studio
Printed in China by 1010 Printing International Limited